The Exeter Family Study

Family breakdown and its impact on children

Monica Cockett
Research Fellow

and

John Tripp
Senior Lecturer in Child Health

Department of Child Health
Postgraduate Medical School
University of Exeter

UNIVERSITY
of
EXETER
PRESS

99-236859 (1)

Published by
University of Exeter Press

ISBN 0 85989 473 8

This edition first published 1994
Reprinted 1996

The Joseph Rowntree Foundation has supported this project as
part of its programme of research and innovative
development projects, which it hopes will be of value to policy
makers and practitioners. The facts presented and views
expressed in this report, however, are those of the authors
and not necessarily those of the Foundation.

SUPPORTED BY

JR

**JOSEPH
ROWNTREE
FOUNDATION**

Design and print by Intertype

Contents

Acknowledgements 4

chapter 1   **Introduction 5**

chapter 2   **The families 8**

chapter 3   **Parental circumstances 11**

chapter 4   **Outcomes for children 18**

chapter 5   **Divorce 41**

chapter 6   **Services 48**

chapter 7   **Discussion 53**

chapter 8   **Recommendations 61**

Appendix 1   Previous research 66

Appendix 2   Methods 77

Appendix 3   The data 84

Bibliography 91

Acknowledgements

The Department of Child Health, Postgraduate Medical School, University of Exeter, would like to thank the families and children who worked with the Department of Child Health on the Joseph Rowntree Foundation study, and the 13 local schools that were involved in the initial stages of the study.

Thanks are also due to the teachers and family doctors who responded to the school and medical questionnaires.

The department gratefully acknowledges the statistical help received from Dr Clive Lawrence and Dr Nicola Crichton of the Department of Computer Sciences at the University of Exeter, and the invaluable advice and statistical support received throughout the study from Dr Diana Kuh of the Department of Community Medicine, University College, London.

The research team included Lisa Baxter, Liz Corney and Margaret Scott, who carried out the interviews, and Gill Creber, who assisted with the coding and checking of the questionnaires. Dr Mohamed Amooie carried out work on the data and analysis, produced the graphics for the report and for presentations.

The manuscript was typed by Debbie Perry and Lindsay Buchanan, and we thank them for their patience and kindness during numerous redraftings. We also thank the staff of the Department of Child Health for their constant support.

The department has also received advice and support from the Advisory Group convened at the beginning of the study; this has proved invaluable. The members of the Advisory Group were: Diane Chorley, HMI, London; Dr Masud Hoghughi, The Aycliffe Centre, Durham; Lisa Parkinson, Director of the Family Mediation Association; Dr Martin Richards, Institute of Child Health, University of Cambridge; Dr Majorie Smith, The Thomas Coram Foundation, London and Dr Mike Wadsworth, Department of Community Medicine, University College, London. We greatly appreciate their comments, support and advice throughout the study.

The Department of Child Health gratefully acknowledges the financial support of the Joseph Rowntree Foundation, and the editorial and general support of its Press Officer, David Utting.

Monica Cockett
Dr John H Tripp

November 1994

Introduction

"We were like any other couple, we argued about sex, money and the kids, yet I didn't think it would end. I should have stayed; and then afterwards she wouldn't have me back."
Interview with a non-resident father

Background

The traditional image of a family is of two parents and their "two point two" children. Social, legal and financial systems continue to uphold this view, yet the reality for the one in three families in England who experience breakdown is often very different. Nor does the growing mis-match between public expectations and private experience help parents and children in their efforts to reorganise their lives after marital breakdown.

Family change

One consequence of the changing pattern of family structures during the past 25 years has been a rise in the number of lone parent households, mainly headed by women. These now account for one in five families with dependent children. Six out of ten lone parent households are the result of divorce. Forty per cent of all children born in 1991 were born outside marriage, nearly 30 per cent of whom were born to cohabiting rather than to married parents.[1] Despite the fact that so many marriages now fail, the number of couples who approach a first marriage with optimism has not been seriously affected.[2] Nor have the increasingly large numbers, who are distressed and surprised when their first marriage does not last, been deterred from repeating the process for a second time. However, seven out of ten divorcees now choose to cohabit before they marry again.[3]

The Children Act (1989)

The Children Act (1989) has required a fundamental shift in the approach of services working with families that experience disruption. One basic concept of the Act is that parental responsibility for children remains firmly with both parents. The rule applies in almost all circumstances, except when this conflicts with the best interests of the child. This has important implications for families experiencing separation and divorce, as both parents are now expected to take equal responsibility for their children after the marriage has ended, and even in circumstances where the child or children live with only one parent for most of the time.[4]

Prior to the Children Act, one parent – usually the mother – had custody of the child. Care and control usually went to the parent with custody, while access rights were given to the non-resident parent. Under the new legislation, no court orders are to be made about contact or residence provided that parents can agree about plans for their children. It is assumed that parents will negotiate. The Act also underlines the need for those making decisions about children to listen to children, so that their wishes can be taken into account when deciding what is in their best interests. In some situations what children want to happen may be very different to what adults think is best for them.[5]

Divorce reform

Before 1973, divorce was based on the concept of a "guilty party", with one partner usually accused of adultery. The reforms of 20 years ago[6] made divorce dependent on the irretrievable breakdown of the marriage, demonstrated in one of five possible ways, including separation by consent for 2 years. However, the majority of divorces in England and Wales go through in as little as 6 months, and are still based on the "unreasonable behaviour" or adultery of one or other partner. This requires long descriptions of one partner's misdemeanours to be passed between solicitors and cannot be expected to help parents to work together to make decisions about their children's future.

It was this situation which led to the Law Commission's proposals for further reform in 1990.[7] This was followed by the publication of a consultation paper by the Lord Chancellor suggesting that "no fault" divorce be made available, but only after a 1 year period for reflection and possible reconciliation. If it was clear that the marriage had broken-down irretrievably, mediation could take place between the partners to help them resolve a division of their property and to plan together for their children's future.[8]

Child support

The Government has, meanwhile, become concerned about the cost of supporting children whose parents have divorced, but where the absent parent (usually the father) no longer supports the family financially. This led to the setting up of the Child Support Agency in 1993, responsible for assessing and collecting the absent parent's contribution towards child maintenance.

This agency ran into practical difficulties in its first year, as well as attracting criticism of its methods and doubts as to its rationale. (Questions were asked about whether its function was to make life better for families or simply to save taxpayers' money.) There are fears that its activities may have the unwelcome side-effect of shifting poverty from first families to step-families.

The Exeter family study

In a context of changing social structures and changing legislation, the present pilot study interviewed parents and children in Exeter about their experiences of living in different kinds of family. This report is the result of talking to 152 children from to two age groups (9–10 and 13–14) and to their parents. Half the children were living with both their biological parents in "intact" families and half lived in families that had been "re-ordered" by parental separation or divorce.[9] Among this latter group, the actual separation or divorce had occurred more than 5 years before the time of interview for 34 of the children, between 4 and 5 years earlier for 32 of the children, and less than 4 years earlier for ten children, five of whom were within 1 year of separation.

Aims of the Study

The principal aims of the study were to:

- Look at the kinds of structures that children experience as "family".

- See what kinds of networks families maintain amongst their relatives.

- See whether children who have experienced separation and divorce present significantly different health, social and educational profiles – and if so, in what areas.

- Examine the arrangements made for families after separation and divorce and to obtain children's views of arrangements for visiting their non-resident parent.

- Learn which services families and children have used for support or advice, particularly at the time of separation and divorce and to obtain their views.

- Ask whether parents and children could identify other services that might have helped if they had been available.

A major intention was to listen carefully to "the voice of the child". Relatively few studies have sought the views of children in late childhood and early adolescence about their life experiences,[10] problems and needs, or attempted to relate these to family change.[11] Even fewer studies have obtained contemporaneous views from children, their resident and non-resident parents and from professionals involved with their day-to-day lives.[12] No studies that we are aware of have, until now, attempted do this with a sample of families representative of, and drawn from, the general population.

Methods

As a pilot study, one important aim was to find out if it was possible to make contact with children as well as parents, to talk to them about any problems they might have encountered as a result of family change.

Initially, almost 1,000 questionnaires were sent out to families, through 13 schools in the study area. Eventual participants in the study were selected in "matched pairs", where one child had lived with both biological parents but had subsequently experienced family restructuring, and the other child had lived continuously with both biological parents.

The pairs of children were matched according to age, sex, mother's educational background, birth order, whether they attended a state or independent school and social class (head of current household's occupation). These characteristics were chosen because they might otherwise have masked or over-emphasised important differences between the groups. Maternal education was chosen, for example, as an indicator that would match the likely quality of parenting in the original, natural parent family.[13] Other research has shown that levels of parental educational attainment is linked to parenting abilities and skills[14] and influences their socialisation values.[15] This in turn can affect children's behavioural responses.

As the database from which all the families were selected contained responses from over 70 per cent of the random population sampled in a defined geographical area, the re-ordered families can be considered a random sample of such families. The intact families were matched on variables that were largely stable and independent of family change, so that they can be considered a random sample of the (much larger) number of intact families living in the Exeter area. The sample was also stratified to include roughly equal numbers of children who had experienced divorce or separation before or after the age of five and of households where the head was engaged in manual or non-manual work. A full account of the methodology can be found in Appendix 2.

The in-depth, confidential interviews with parents and children, which were conducted by experienced social workers, took place during 1991-2. Children's permission to be interviewed was obtained through their parents. They were not pressed to take part or provide answers to any questions that they did not wish to discuss. Additional data on the families was obtained, with their permission, from schools and from family doctors. The study was, thus, able to measure and compare a number of health, educational and social "outcomes" for children living in different types of family.

1   OPCS. Marriage and Divorce Statistics (1989)

2   Capron, D. (1994) A review of 1992; Population Trends 75. OPCS

3   Kiernan, K. & Estaugh, V. (1993)

4   Critics say that a main fault lies in the fact that the Act assumes that *all* parents are capable of carrying out their responsibilities towards their children equally and in most circumstances. In practice this is not always possible.

5   The 1989 United Nations Charter on the Rights of the Child specifically lays down the implicit rights of the child to have basic needs met: a right to a place to live and to education and health care. It also states that the child has a right to see both parents, and that the child's voice should be heard

6   Matrimonial Causes Act (1973)

7   Law Commission (1990)

8   Lord Chancellor's Department (1993) Consultation Paper

9   It should be noted that the Child Support Act (implemented in 1993), the philosophy behind the Children Act (1989) and the current consideration being given to divorce reform did not have any impact on orders made for the families in the present study

Structure of the report

The families who took part in the pilot study are described further in Chapter 2. Chapter 3 **details the comparisons and outcome differences that were observed from interviews with parents. The detailed results obtained from talking to children are recorded in** Chapter 4, **followed by a discussion of possible causes and effects.**

The experiences of those families who had been through the divorce process are described in Chapter 5, **while** Chapters 6 **examines the use which re-ordered families had made of different services at the time of divorce and views as to their adequacy and room for improvement.**

The implications of the study's findings and a number of recommendations regarding the help and support that children and parents should receive at times of marital stress and separation are summarised in Chapter 7 **and** Chapter 8.

Details of previous research can be found in Appendix 1. **A detailed description of the study methodology appears in** Appendix 2 **and comparative tables setting out the survey data are in** Appendix 3.

10   Mitchell, A. (1985) and Walzak, Y. & Burns, S. (1984) in the UK. Dunlop, R. & Burns, A. (1988) in Australia and Amato, P. (1987) in the USA

11   Hetherington, Cox & Cox (1986); Peterson & Zill (1986); Kiernan et al. (1991); Elliott & Richards (1992)

12   Wallerstein & Kelly (1980). Studies carried out in the UK on clinical and non-clinical samples report similar findings to those of Wallerstein & Kelly reported in *Surviving the Breakup* (1980). The importance of American longitudinal studies is that they encourage similar work in the UK, where there are very different cultural social and economic factors affecting family life. The more liberal influences of 1980s California may have affected American outcomes

13   Kuh, D. & Maclean, M. (1990)

14   See Zill's chapter in *Impact of Divorce, Single Parenting and Step-parenting on Children*, E.M. Hetherington & J.D. Arasteh (Eds), pp. 325–368 for a discussion about levels of parental educational attainment linked to family type

15   Hernandez, D. (1988) in *Impact of Divorce, Single Parenting, and Step-parenting on Children*, E.M. Hetherington & J.D. Arasteh (Eds), pp. 3–22. Hernandez discusses levels of parental education attained and their influences on parenting skills and attitudes to child rearing

The Families

The matched pairs of children and their families in the Exeter Study created two equal-sized samples:

1 Children who were normally resident in a family that had been re-ordered because of the departure of one parent since the child's birth.

2 Children who were normally resident with both their biological parents.

However, the study design allowed further useful comparisons of the way that children in contrasting family circumstances were faring by sub-dividing each group. The re-ordered families were divided into three sub-groups:

1 **Lone parent families** where the child had lived since the separation or divorce of its biological parents.

2 **Step-families** where the child's resident biological parent was living with a new partner (either married or cohabiting) for the first time since separating from the non-resident parent.

3 **Re-disrupted families** where the resident natural parent's re-partnership(s) had broken down. (This group could be further sub-divided between children living with a lone parent and those living in a subsequent step-family).

Intact families were divided into two sub-groups:

1 **Low conflict families** where parents reported no serious rows and no marital problems.

2 **High conflict families** where parents reported rows and/or marital problems.

It was also possible to sub-divide children in the re-ordered families, between those living with two parents or partners and those living with one

---

Table 2.1 **The composition of family (parent figures) where the child interviewed was normally resident**

Who the children lived with		Number
1. *Both biological parents*		
Row Level 1: Reported happy relationship and no rows		41
Row Level 2: Reported rows or unhappy}	22}	
Row Level 3: Reported unhappy and rows}	13}	35
2. *Biological mother*		
(i) Living with new partner		
a) remarried		17
b) divorced with partner		11
c) separated with partner		2
(ii) Living alone		
a) divorced		31
b) separated		8
3. *Biological father*		
a) remarried		1
b) divorced with partner		2
c) separated without partner		3
4. *Neither parent*		1
Total		**152**

parent. However, the first sub-division described above concerning both intact and re-ordered families was used for the main analysis because it identified the family transitions through which children had passed, and made it possible to examine the effects of multiple-disruption. Table 2.1 shows in more detail how the sample of families in the study was made-up.

The sample group of families was even more varied than Table 2.1 suggests. It ranged from children living with both biological parents or living alone with one parent to those who were living with grandparents or aunts and uncles plus one parent. There were 19 children who had experienced two or more changes of parental figure in their lives, and one child who lived with neither natural parent. Three families reported that step-parents and non-resident parents supported each other emotionally and even baby-sat for each other occasionally, but this was unusual.

Intact families were inclined to apologise for their ordinariness: "*You will find us very boring, we like each other and we are thankful for what we have got – a home, children and my mother living close by is all I ever wanted.*" In the researchers' experience, "ordinariness" usually meant that there was:

- Reasonable satisfaction about finance and housing, regardless of socio-economic status.

- Satisfaction with the sharing of tasks and responsibilities in the family.

- Family outings, events and rituals were central to the development of a recognised family "culture" for the children.

- The different needs of each parent and the children were a positive rather than a destructive force.

There were, however, a minority of intact families who, because of ill health, unemployment or family relationship problems, would not describe themselves as "ordinary". Twenty-two of the 35 families in the high conflict group reported having had serious marital and family problems, either now or in the past.

Re-ordered families were more likely to say that their family arrangements were abnormal: "*You won't find more unusual than we are*" or else chose to explain a new partner as a lodger, a landlord or just "a friend". The diversity of family structures experienced by children in re-ordered families is shown in Table 2.2.

Table 2.2 **Family structures (parent figures) of the families where children were resident**				
Intact Families (both natural parents)	76			
Re-ordered Families	76			
First re-ordering	57			
Single parent	-	31		
Mother	-	-	-	28
Father	-	-	-	3
Parent with partner	-	-	26	
Mother + stepfather	-	-	-	15
Mother + partner	-	-	-	8
Father + stepmother	-	-	-	1
Father + partner	-	-	-	2
Second or subsequent re-ordering	-	19		
Single parent (mother)	-	-	10	
Parent with partner	-	-	9	
Mother + stepfather	-	-	-	5
Mother + partner	-	-	-	2
Father + partner	-	-	-	2

One parent families

There were 31 children living in lone parent households following the first marital breakdown: 28 with their natural mothers and three with their natural fathers (two girls and one boy). Five lone mothers had never been married to the child's natural father, though they had cohabited at least until after the child's birth.

In some cases the mothers had formed new relationships but these were not with "live-in" partners, even though they spent some time in the home. Children appeared able to make a clear distinction between the two. Mothers gave a number of reasons for not allowing new relationships to become permanent, including resentment on the part of their child and a conscious decision to remain independent. Three mothers said they had deferred new long-term relationships until their children were older and visited their friends away from the house.

A minority of lone parents interviewed who had been part of a two parent family and had hoped to remain so, said they did not feel themselves to be a "real" family. But for some of the non-resident parents this feeling was even stronger: *"We will never be a family – its just me and the two boys at the weekend, so we are isolated – we cannot join in with other families."* The interviewers also noted such comments from mothers as: *"I never expected to be on my own with the children"* and *"I have all the responsibility"*. Alternatively, as one child commented: *"It feels different with just Mum."*

Step-families

There were 24 children who lived with their natural mother plus her new partner after the first marital breakdown experienced by the child; two children lived with their fathers in a new family. Some families reported general improvement; mothers reported more support, but for others, problems had multiplied: *"There has been constant turmoil since the divorce and remarriage, constant stress."*

Re-disrupted families

"Financial problems can force a second marriage – which could be a mistake."

Ten children were living alone with their natural mother following a second or subsequent marital breakdown: *"I married a second time as a meal ticket and it's never worked out."*

Seven children were living with their mother and her new partner after two or more family transitions, five of whom were re-married and two of whom were cohabiting. One boy lived with his father and three brothers and sisters plus new partner (and child), whom he declined to regard as a parental figure: *"She's all right but her baby is a nuisance."* Another child lived with neither of his natural parents, having stayed with his step-father and his new partner after the break-up of his mother's two previous marriages. From his mother's point of view, this was a relief: *"I am not cut out to be a mother."* From the child's point of view, although he greatly missed his mother, life had settled down: *"Living with her (step-father's new partner) is like being with an older sister, its great."*

The Exeter Family Study

Parental Circumstances

This chapter compares the economic and social well-being of the parents who took part in the study. Its initial conclusions are discussed at the end of the section, but are considered in greater detail following the presentation of data on outcomes for children in Chapter 4.

Note on the use of data

The data and various figures in this report are presented in a format that compares households where children were living in re-ordered families with those of matched children in intact families. Comparisons have also been made between different sub-groups:

The majority of figures are presented as follows:

- **The re-ordered families were divided into those where children were living with a lone parent following their parent's divorce or separation ("first-time" lone parent families), those whose resident parent had "re-partnered" and were living in step-families for the first time, and those living in families where they had "lost" a parent on two or more occasions ("re-disrupted" families).**

- **The intact families were subdivided into two groups according to whether the relationship between parents was reportedly characterised by high or low levels of conflict.**

The figures in Chapter 3 and 4 (except 3.1, 4.5, 4.6, 4.7) are arranged in the following way: from histograms and data columns from left to right are: all intact families followed by intact families divided into low/high conflict groups (columns 1, 2, 3); all re-ordered families divided into single, step and re-disrupted family groups (columns 4, 5, 6, 7).

An odds ratio was calculated by comparing "outcome" results for different sub-groups with those for their matched pairs. These indicate whether differences between the various groups are statistically significant, i.e. the probability that they are unlikely to have occurred by chance. Various degrees of statistical significance are shown on the figures in this chapter using asterisks (* = $P < 0.05$; ** = $P < 0.01$; *** = $P < 0.001$). Statistical significance for all intact (column 1) not shown since it is identical to all re-ordered (column 4).

A fuller methodological note can be found in Appendix 2. Tables describing the numbers of matched pairs, discordant pairs and odd ratios for each outcome are shown in Appendix 3.

A small number of figures are divided in different ways to illustrate the data and separate explanations are given in the text.

Income

Parents were asked to estimate their levels of weekly household income, excluding Child Benefit and maintenance, but including Income Support, Family Credit and any Invalidity Benefits. Only 4 per cent of intact families had an income of less than £90 per week, compared with 22 per cent of re-ordered families. Eighteen per cent of intact families and 24 per cent of re-ordered families had an income of less than £135 per week, and 27 per cent of intact families and 18 per cent of re-ordered families had an income of up to £150. Incomes of over £150 per week were found among 51 per cent of the intact families and 35 per cent of the re-ordered families. (Income levels could not be determined for 4 per cent of intact families and 6 per cent of re-ordered families.)

Dual earners

In 71 per cent of intact families both parents undertook paid work, compared with just 24 per cent of the re-ordered families. All but two of these were in the step-family sub-group, where 62 per cent had two incomes.

Maintenance

While just over half (54 per cent) of re-ordered families received some financial support from the non-resident parent, only one in five (21 per cent) received regular maintenance payments which could be relied on. Fifty-eight per cent of lone parents, 54 per cent of the step-family group and 47 per cent of the re-disrupted group said that they received *some* support from the non-resident parent. (Six out of ten who were in receipt of maintenance were being paid more than £10 per week for the family).[1] Among the step-families, 31 per cent were receiving maintenance payments *and* had two incomes. The two dual earner families in the re-disrupted group also received regular maintenance.[2]

Table 3.1 **Receipt of Social Security benefits**

	Intact Families	Re-ordered Families
Income Support	6	27
Unemployment	4	2
Family Credit	3	8
Disability/invalidity	1	3
One Parent Benefit	0	8
Totals:	14	45*

* Three families receiving two benefits.

Benefit

Of the 59 families receiving Social Security benefits, 45 were re-ordered and 14 were intact (Table 3.1). Among re-ordered families, step-families were less likely to be receiving benefits and lone parents more so (Figure 3.1a).

Feeling "worse off"

Although 46 per cent of re-ordered families describe their financial status as "worse" after family change, other parents reported positive outcomes. Some 41 per cent regarded themselves as better off, either because they had more control over their finances or because they had benefited from a new partner's income (Figure 3.1). The remainder (13 per cent) felt that there was little difference.

Although lone parents, including those receiving benefit, often felt they had better control of their finances than when married or cohabiting, because they were able to account for their spending themselves, they were still more likely to regard themselves as worse off than either step-families or intact families (Figure 3.1b).

Figure 3.1 **Figure 3.1A, 3.1B, 3.1C, 3.1D show from left to right: all intact families (1st column) and re-ordered families, divided into single and step-family groups (2nd and 3rd columns). The next four columns show these step and single family groups divided according to the first and second re-ordering (4, 5, 6, 7th columns).**

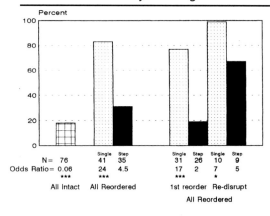

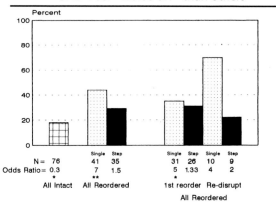

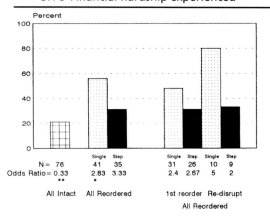

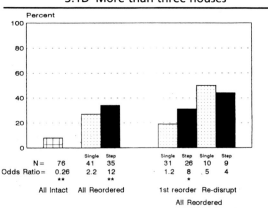

The Exeter Family Study

Financial hardship

Parents in re-ordered families were more likely to say that they had gone without things they really needed during the past year (Figure 3.1c).

Holidays

Intact families were more likely to have taken a holiday during the past year (61 per cent) than re-ordered families (46 per cent). Children in intact homes were also more likely to have been away with members of their extended family, such as aunts, cousins and grandparents. There was little difference between the step- and lone parent groups, although the step-families were slightly more likely to resemble intact families. The re-disrupted families were least likely to have taken a break.

Cars

Only 13 per cent of intact families had no car compared with 42 per cent of single parent families while step-parent families were very similar to intact families – with 8 per cent having no personal transport. Nearly one-third of intact families (32 per cent) owned two cars, compared to 23 per cent of step-families, no single parent families and 5 per cent of re-disrupted families. Transport difficulties were found to affect the families' social networks; some said they had not been into the centre of Exeter for months because of transport costs. A minority of children in both the intact and re-ordered families spent their school holidays playing in and around their own neighbourhood because of lack of finance and transport for family outings.

Pocket money

Most children, regardless of socio-economic status or family type, were given regular sums or could ask if they needed money. The resident parent usually provided this, with the non-resident parent occasionally giving money as an extra.

Housing

The way that families were selected in matched pairs meant that differences in housing status between the intact and re-ordered families in the study were less pronounced than might be expected in a sample of the general population. Three out of four intact families (75 per cent) were owner-occupiers compared with 56 per cent of re-ordered families. One in five intact families were council tenants (20 per cent) compared with one in three (30 per cent) re-ordered families.

However, divorcing families who had owned their own homes were more likely to have suffered a reduction in housing status. In some cases the resident parent and children had remained in the family home, but it was more usual for the house to have been sold and a smaller, cheaper property purchased. For the non-resident parent, meanwhile, divorce had almost always meant a loss of housing status. However, one in four who had formed a new, live-in relationship had regained their previous quality of life because of their new partner's contribution towards housing costs.

Moves

Re-ordered families were more likely than intact families to have moved house more than three times since birth, but step and re-disrupted families had had the most changes of address (Figure 3.1d).

Needs

Levels of satisfaction with housing were similar for intact families and first-time step-families, who tended to see the need for improvements in terms of another bedroom, a bigger garden, or "living in a better neighbourhood". The housing needs of lone parent and re-disrupted families were often more basic: proper heating, dealing with dampness in bedrooms and finding the money for renovation and re-decoration. Shortage of bedroom space was a common problem in two-parent families (see Appendix 3, Table 1).

Family organisation

Parents were asked about how they and their partners shared household tasks, including caring for the children and enforcing family rules and discipline. Mothers in re-ordered families were asked how these responsibilities had been arranged in their marriage or cohabitation with the study child's father as well as during any current relationship (see Appendix 3, Table 1).

It was found that parents in intact families tended to set more rules for their children and express higher levels of satisfaction about family organisation than those in re-ordered families.[3] Both parents and children reported that family organisation and responsibility had changed after separation or divorce, with most parents feeling that they were less strict with their children.[4]

Mothers in re-ordered families reported that domestic tasks were less likely to have been shared in either their current or previous relationships, with consequent levels of dissatisfaction (Figures 3.2 and 3.3). It was, however, apparent that the description of "who did what" provided by resident parents differed from that provided by non-resident parents, who more frequently insisted that the tasks had been shared.

Child care

Mothers in re-ordered families reported having the main responsibility for child care (75 per cent)

Figure 3.2 **Resident parent's dissatisfaction with the sharing of household tasks and responsibilities (current or subsequent relationship)**

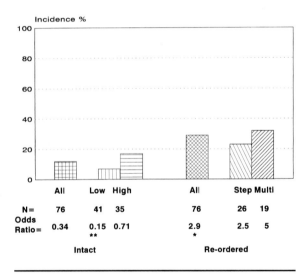

Figure 3.3 **Resident parent's dissatisfaction with the sharing of household tasks and responsibilities in the original relationship**

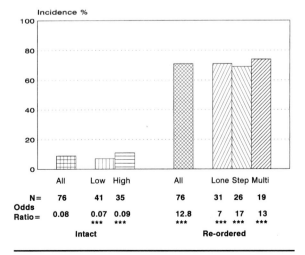

and making decisions about the children, with little reported sharing of roles. Intact families reported a much higher proportion of shared responsibility and less dissatisfaction with their arrangements, although levels of satisfaction were reduced in intact families where there was a high level of conflict (Figure 3.2).

Parental health

Parents were asked to describe the overall state of their health and were questioned about specific health problems, whether they were currently visiting their doctor and about their smoking and drinking habits. They were also invited to say whether they thought their own health problems had affected their children and whether they linked their state of health to family change.5

Altogether, 31 parents reported problems with their general health, with those in re-ordered families (20) more likely to be experiencing difficulties.[6] They were also less likely to be satisfied with their health care (see Appendix 3, Table 2).

Nerves

Thirty parents said they had current problems with "nerves" and 48 reported problems in the past. Twenty-four parents in re-ordered families reported difficulties, compared to just six in the intact families (Figure 3.4).[7] There was little difference between the experience of parents high conflict and low conflict intact families. Nor, within the higher incidence of problems reported among re-ordered families, was there much difference between lone parents, step-parents and parents in re-disrupted families. A comparison between resident and non-resident parents in 27 re-ordered families found nearly all of them reported problems with sleep, tiredness or nerves (24 resident, 22 non-resident).[8]

More re-ordered family parents said they had suffered problems with their nerves in the past than parents in intact families (Figure 3.5). However, parents living in (first-time) step-families recalled fewer difficulties than lone parents and those in re-disrupted families, as compared to intact controls.

Parents who reported problems with their nerves commonly associated these psychological and psychosomatic difficulties with family change and re-organisation. Among the re-ordered families, both the resident and non-resident parents associated health and other problems with their separation. More resident parents (16)

Figure 3.4 **Parents' report of current problem with nerves**

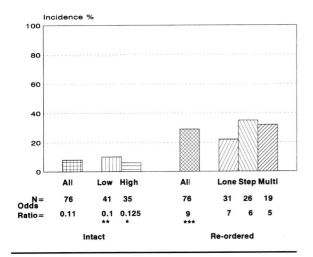

Figure 3.4 **Parents' report of current problem with nerves**

reported "problems with nerves" than the non-resident parents (9) but among the latter there were one or two fathers who said they had been so badly affected as to be unable to work at the time of separation: *"I didn't know what to expect, I drifted from week to week living on booze and chips. I lived only for weekends, when I saw the children."*

GP visits

Only slightly more parents in re-ordered families were currently visiting their family doctor (35), compared with those in intact families (27). Parents in the "re-disrupted" group were most likely to have recently attended the surgery. There were no obvious differences between the reasons given by intact and re-ordered families for needing to see their GP. Equal numbers of parents in the intact and re-ordered groups – just over a third – were currently taking prescribed

medication (excluding the contraceptive pill). However, half the parents in the re-disrupted sub-group were taking medication.

Smoking and drinking

About a third of parents in the study were smokers, but parents in re-ordered families were more likely to report that they smoked, both currently and in the past. Some 7 per cent of parents in intact families, compared with 26 per cent in re-ordered families, described themselves as being heavy smokers in the past. There was little difference between lone and re-disrupted families in the reported numbers smoking, but step-families were more like intact families in their habits.

Most parents consumed alcohol (84 per cent). Four per cent (3) of parents in intact families and 14 per cent (11) in re-ordered families, described themselves as "having a drink problem" in the past. Eleven non-resident parents placed themselves in this category, compared with four resident parents.[9]

Children affected by their parents' health

In all, 68 parents reported feeling that their own health problems had affected the child being studied by the research. Parents in re-ordered families had more health problems and were more likely to think that they had a negative effect on their child (Figure 3.6). This was especially true of lone parents and those who had experienced the breakdown of two or more relationships. Step-parents, in this respect, were more like their matched pairs in intact families.

Figure 3.5 **Parents' report of past problem with nerves**

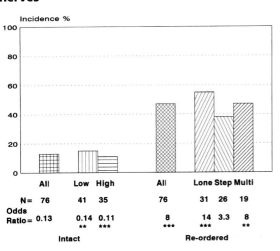

Figure 3.6 **Parents' perception that their health problems had adverse effects on their child**

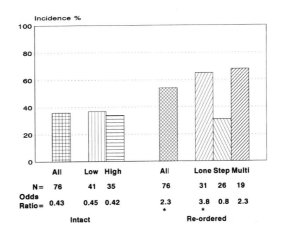

Children's concern for their parents

Fourteen per cent (11) children in intact families, compared with 22 per cent (17) in re-ordered families, were concerned about their mother's smoking or drinking. A rather higher proportion of children expressed concerns for their fathers – 17 per cent (13) in intact families and 27 per cent (21) of those in re-ordered families.[10]

Social life

Parents in re-ordered families were, overall, slightly more likely to be worried about their social life than those in intact families. They reported that a lack of money, shortage of baby sitters and disapproval from grandparents, were among the inhibiting factors[11] (Figure 3.7).

Intact families, although they experienced similar constraints, also reported disagreements about the mother's lack of social life and her dissatisfaction with "father going out alone". Children in intact families reported that problems about "Dad going to the pub" and "Dad working too much" were a particular cause of parental rows.

Parents in intact families went out less frequently than those in re-ordered families, but were more likely to say that they stayed in "happily", and were not actively seeking a social life outside the home. Parents in intact families (and in a minority of re-ordered families), were also more likely to regard their social activities, including sport, as outings for the whole family, rather than for their individual enjoyment.

Resident parents reported more problems with their social life than non-resident parents

(16 versus 7). Most were mothers, who may have found it more difficult to establish new social networks than their ex-partners. They reported more financial restraints on their social life, as well as a lack of transport and having to make childcare arrangements: "We've all had to accept a lower standard of living since the divorce." Some said they now tried to take part in social and sporting activities with their children rather than pursue a separate social life of their own. Lone parents reported the most dissatisfaction with their social life compared with the child's non-resident parent.[12]

Some non-resident parents maintained they went out more often because they "had nothing else to do", but also complained that their jobs and lack of finance limited their social life.[13] However, a quarter of resident and non-resident parents reported that their social life was better, especially where they had met new partners whose social interests matched their own.

Discussion

It is generally recognised that re-ordered families are less well off than intact families. It was, therefore, to be expected that the examination of socio-economic factors among families in the Exeter study would find that (in all circumstances) intact families reported fewer problems than re-ordered families.

In this study, however (as in others), greater financial security was associated with the presence of two adults, rather than one, in the family.[14] Thus, while almost all the re-ordered families had been significantly worse off (at least for a period) following separation, it was the lone parent sub-group that was much more likely to be receiving social security benefits, to have gone without things they really needed, or to feel generally "worse off".

The re-disrupted sub-group of families contained both lone and step-families, who were generally worse-off than the equivalent families that had undergone only one re-ordering.

Step-families were more like intact families than one parent families in terms of finance, transport and holidays. Nevertheless, in spite of being objectively better-off financially, it was evident that step-family parents often felt hard pressed by their commitments following the amalgamation of two families.

Re-ordered families were also more likely to report problems with nerves, both now and in the past, though there was little difference between the numbers of parents in re-ordered or intact

Figure 3.7 **Parental dissatisfaction with social life**

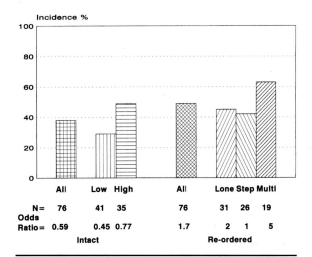

The Exeter Family Study

families who were currently visiting their GP. Intact families, though they may not have had very active social lives, reported less dissatisfaction. Re-ordered families reported more financial constraints on their socialising, particularly lone parent families.

1   Bradshaw, J. et al. (1991).

2   Eekelaar, J. & Maclean, M. (1986).

3   Mansfield, P. & Collard, J. (1988) The Beginning Of The Rest Of Your Life. In this study intact families were also likely to be more satisfied with sharing household tasks.

4   Wallerstein, J. & Kelly, J. (1980); Capaldi, D, et al (1991); Hetherington, EM. et al (1992). These studies reported a diminished ability by parents to cope at the acute stage of family breakdown, as reported by some parents in this study; there was also a recorded improvement over time with some parents and children preferring the new routine (e.g. children could bring friends home more freely, etc.).

5   Kuh, D. & Maclean, M. (1990). This paper based on the 1946 cohort study and shows that there was an increased risk for women whose parents had been divorced to drink and smoke more than women whose parents remained married to each other.

6   Dominian, J. et al. (1991) In a reply to the Department of Health document, Health of the Nation, these researchers reported a greater risk of health difficulties for men and women who had experienced divorce.

7   See also Chester, R. (1973) re: over-representation of divorcing/ divorced parents in doctors' waiting rooms and hospital outpatient departments.

8   See Hetherington, EM. (1986); Wallerstein, J. & Kelly, J. (1980); Kiernan, K. (1992) re: ill health affecting parent's ability to parent, especially in the early days of family breakdown.

9   See Kuh, D. & Maclean, M. (1990).

10 See Wadsworth, M. (1991); Hetherington, E.M. et al. (1978, 1979, 1986); Wallerstein, J. & Kelly, J. (1980); Dominian, J. et al. (1991) re: the effects on parental health of separation and divorce.

11 A small group of parents in re-ordered families had become involved with Gingerbread – a support group for divorced parents, and had enjoyed activities organised for the children. Some had even met new partners. A minority of non-resident parents felt discriminated against, as they were not allowed to join the local group because their ex-partner was already a member (see Appendix 3, Table 1).

12 Bradshaw, J. et al. (1991) reports the effect of low income on the social activities of parents and children, especially in lone parent families.

13 See also Wallerstein, J. & Kelly, J. (1980) Surviving the Breakup for qualitative accounts of resident and non-resident parents limited social life due to lowered income, which was also reported in this study.

14 See Burghes, L. (1993); Jacobs, J. & Furstenberg, F. (1986), whose studies show that two parent households, whether first time married or remarried, are financially more secure than lone parent families or re-disrupted families.

4 Outcomes for Children

"I have been amazed at how resilient they are, even though they were both upset."

Resident mother

This chapter compares and contrasts the experience of children living in different family groups. It considers the effects that family change may have had on their health, their sense of well-being, their friendships with other children and their school work. It also examines their relationships with parents and other members of their extended families. Quite sensitive indicators[1] are used to measure different "outcomes" to discover which children had generally fared better and which worse. Parents' assessments are considered alongside those of the children themselves.

The 9- and 10-year-olds who took part in the study were at an age where past research suggested that any problems at school or in the home might start to become entrenched. The 13- and 14-year-olds who were interviewed were of an age where problems might either be expected to dissipate or to become more overt.

Children in both age groups proved very willing to talk to the research team, either with their parents present or, in most instances, on their own. From the outset it was obvious that, for some children, little in their lives was causing them concern. Others had run into problems that were often, but not always, echoed by their parents. In either case, the children were remarkably clear about the important matters of fact in their lives and in describing their feelings about change.

Protective Factors

There is no dispute that conflict between parent with or without separation and divorce, is a major stress, usually producing short, medium and long term adverse outcomes for children; these however are not universal and it is important to recognise that children and families are individuals and interactions between personality, relationships and outside influences are unique.

In his studies, Rutter[2] proposes that because outcomes for individuals placed in very similar circumstances are so variable, it is important to consider not only the factors influencing transition but also the processes, and that these have an individual basis for each person. Previous life experiences as well as "nature" (equivalent to personality, etc.) have important effects on the direction of changes in life trajectory and may occur with major events, so that chain effects are commonly important in determining whether the result is towards risk or adaptation.

Longitudinal studies have indicated that there are long term negative results for some children following their parents' separation and divorce, with an indication of lowered future life chances. Failure at school has been highlighted[3] as being one of the chief predictors of future life chances, i.e. less chance of entry into higher education and lowered employment opportunities.

One of the aims of the study was to try to find indications of ways that would reduce the numbers of children who were reporting difficulties in the long term.

Well-being and self-esteem

"She was openly upset and tearful after the separation, now often angry and resentful but slowly improving"

Happiness

Two out of three parents reported that their child was usually happy (Figure 4.1). Parents in re-ordered families were more likely to report that their child was sometimes, or often, unhappy.

This concern extended to children who appeared abnormally quiet or withdrawn, as well as to more obvious manifestations of misery (see Appendix 3, Table 3). In all, 29 parents from re-ordered families reported problems compared with 11 from intact families. Interestingly, it was parents who had re-partnered and were living in step-families who were significantly more likely to report that their children had problems, compared with parents in intact families.[4]

More children in re-ordered families described themselves as unhappy than in the intact families (Figure 4.2), and there was a slightly higher rate of

Figure 4.1 **Parents' description of their child as sometimes or often unhappy**

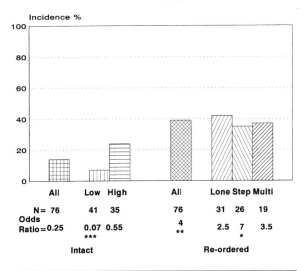

Figure 4.2 **Children's reports of being sometimes or often unhappy**

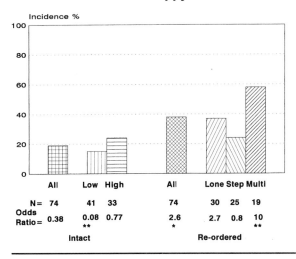

unhappiness in the intact families marked by high levels of conflict. Children in the low-conflict families were significantly different in terms of their personal happiness compared with those in re-ordered families.

The higher incidence of children who described themselves as unhappy was most marked in the re-disrupted group. By contrast, the incidence of reported unhappiness was similar among children in step- and intact families and not significantly different to that among children living (for the first time) in a one parent family.[5] A difference, therefore, existed between the perceptions of parents in step-families – who were particularly likely to be concerned that their children were unhappy – and the feelings that children themselves reported. Conversely, parents in re-disrupted families appeared more complacent (or unaware) as to their children's well-being than the children themselves.[6]

Self-esteem

"It doesn't take a lot to make her cry."

The study used the Rosenberg self-image scale[7] as a further test of children's feelings. Half the children displayed good self-esteem, but children in high-conflict, intact families were rather less likely to show good self-esteem than those where conflict was low. However, children in re-ordered families were significantly more likely to report lower self-esteem than their matched pair in an intact family. Negative factors were reported by children from 44 re-ordered families compared with 23 intact families. In particular, children from re-ordered families were less likely to say they were "satisfied with myself" or feel "positive" about themselves (Figure 4.3).

The difference in odds ratios between step-parent families and their matched pairs was not statistically significant (see Appendix 3, Table 3).[8]

"Some days I do really well and other days when I get muddled I don't do so well."

A scale devised by the Department of Child Health (see Appendix 3) was also applied to ascertain children's sense of self-worth and how they thought others viewed them. It found that those in re-ordered families were more likely to say that they felt awkward in company, that they did not like meeting new people or that they were concerned about what other people thought about them. On this measurement, children in high-conflict intact families more closely resembled children in lone parent and (first-time) step-families than those in the low-conflict intact

Figure 4.3 **Children's view of their own self-worth as measured on the Rosenberg scale**

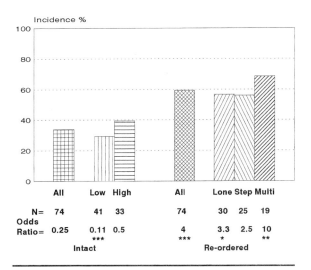

Figure 4.4 **Children's view of their own social image (eg how other people viewed them) as measured using a derived scale**

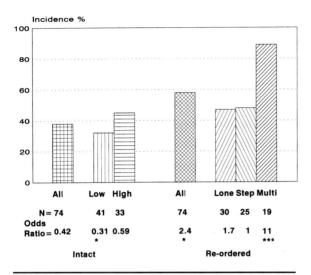

	All	Low	High	All	Lone	Step	Multi
N =	74	41	33	74	30	25	19
Odds Ratio =	0.42	0.31 *	0.59	2.4 *	1.7	1	11 ***
		Intact			Re-ordered		

families. But children in re-disrupted families had a significantly poorer sense of their social image than their opposite numbers in intact families (Figure 4.4). In all, 42 re-ordered family children and 28 from intact families recorded a negative view of themselves. The 72 children who felt their ability to be responsible was under-rated were more evenly distributed between the re-ordered families (40) and intact families (32). These children were more likely to suggest that they were not "good" at making decisions and were unhappy about the way other people treated them. Children in re-ordered families were more likely to say that they felt moody or miserable and were less satisfied, overall, with "everyday things".

Self-esteem related to other problems

A factor emerging at this stage is that children who described problems with low self-esteem were also more likely to report difficulties in other areas of their lives. These included general and psychosomatic health problems (see below) as well as unhappiness and a lack of well-being (Figure 4.5). Children suffering from low self-esteem were also more likely to have been referred for psychological or psychiatric help.

Figure 4.5 **The incidence of various health problems in children with low self-esteem**

Figures 4.5, 4.6, 4.7 show the data in the following way:

– all re-ordered families are shown in the back histograms

– all intact families are shown in the front row

– each group is divided into whether the child reported problems with low self-esteem (Y) or otherwise (N)

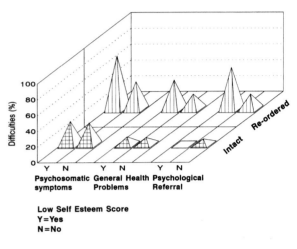

Figure 4.6 **Experience of difficulties at school by children with low self-esteem**

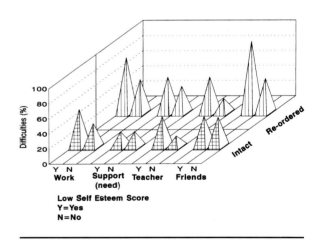

They more often said that they were experiencing problems at school and were more likely to have received extra help with their school work (Figure 4.6).

The same was true of problems with friends and with social lives (Figure 4.7).

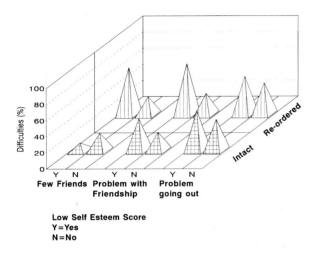

Low Self Esteem Score
Y=Yes
N=No

Children's health

General Health

The health profiles of children living in the different family groups were, in many respects, similar – for instance, as regarded the frequency of infectious diseases and the numbers reporting asthma, eczema and upper respiratory infections. There was also little difference in the numbers of parents in either the intact or re-ordered families who recalled problems with their children at the time of birth or in reaching developmental "milestones" as infants.

However, 27 children in re-ordered families said they had more than three current health problems compared with nine of those in intact families. The most problems were reported by children who had experienced multiple family change. Moreover, whereas 50 children in re-ordered families had visited a family doctor in the last 6 months, the same was true of only 27 in intact families. Children in both family groups reported similar numbers of visits to hospital Accident and Emergency Departments, but children in re-ordered families reported more resulting stays in hospital, suggesting that the accidents were of a more serious nature.[9]

Three re-ordered family children and two from intact families had a categorised physical disability, two of these children had experienced difficulties following orthopaedic surgery. This group of children had particular problems with school work and social life due to hospitalisation,

and (in re-ordered families) also had more overall problems with "social adjustment" at school and reported more problems with self-image (see Appendix 3, Table 4).

Psychosomatic health problems

Problems with children's health reported by parents were classified by the research team as likely to be psychosomatic (or "functional") if children presenting similar symptoms in clinical practice would normally have been given that diagnosis. They included recurrent pains, headaches, stomach aches, feeling sick and other non-specific symptoms.[10]

Figure 4.8 shows that parents in re-ordered families reported more such problems than those in intact families. Among intact families, there was little difference between the parental reports of psychosomatic symptoms between the high and low-conflict sub-groups. More problems were reported by re-ordered families, with the re-disrupted families most noticeably different to their intact family controls. Children in step-families were also more likely to have psychosomatic health problems compared with their matched pair among the intact families.

Children were more likely to report symptoms classified as psychosomatic than their parents – not surprisingly, as a number said there were problems which they had kept to themselves. Once again, symptoms were reported significantly more often by children in re-ordered families than intact families. Children in re-ordered families were also more likely to regard their problems as serious, in the sense that they occurred frequently or interfered with their lives.

Figure 4.8 **Health symptoms and illness reported by parents and classified as likely to be psychosomatic (functional)**

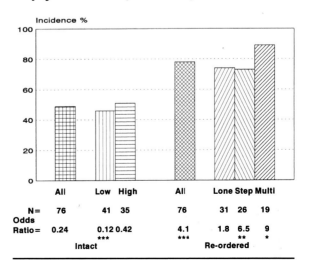

Eating problems

Similar numbers of children in both family groups described themselves as "fussy eaters" including a minority who had more serious problems than just "not liking vegetables". Parents identified six children as having a categorised eating disorder (two in intact families, four in re-ordered), only three of whom had received specialist help. One mother said *"She is 2 stone overweight, but this may not be directly related to changes. I am getting suicidal about her weight."* Another mother related her child's problems to family change and the resulting financial insecurity *"She eats too much because she's afraid of being hungry – like she was when we were on benefits."*

Bed wetting

Twice as many children in re-ordered families (15) as intact families (7) said that they either currently wet the bed or that this had been a problem in the past.[11] One child's problems were associated with the stress of living with both parents in the same house while they planned their divorce. The boy exhibited acute difficulties in other areas of his life.

Soiling

This was only reported by two parents (not by the children themselves). It was associated with acute family stress –in one case the death of the absent father by suicide and in another by the introduction of a new partner into the family.

Psychological and psychiatric referrals

Children in low-conflict intact families were least likely to have had a psychological referral, while children in re-disrupted families reported the highest numbers. Children living in intact families marked by high levels of parental conflict were more likely than those in other intact families to have had a psychological referral, but not to the extent which applied to the re-ordered family groups. Step-families reported fewer referrals than the lone parent and re-disrupted families (Figure 4.9).

Among five children from intact families who had been referred for assessment, one suffered from an eating disorder, two needed support with school work and two required help with "family problems". Among the 20 children in re-ordered

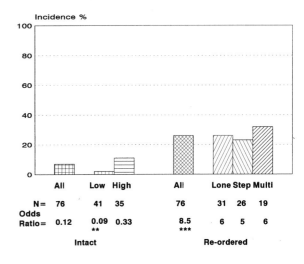

Figure 4.9 **Numbers of children referred to child and adolescent psychology and psychiatry services, or to the educational psychology service**

families who were receiving help, problems included lack of concentration, hyperactivity, eating problems (including failure to thrive), sleeping difficulties, bed-wetting, temper tantrums, panic attacks at school and "chronic anxiety state".

It emerged that a number of parents and children had problems which they regarded as "serious", but which teachers and doctors had not considered worth referring-on. This was true of some children in both intact and re-ordered families, although there were proportionately more difficulties identified in re-ordered families. One mother, looking back to her child's problems at the time of separation said *"I didn't expect the health service to fail us or feel incapable of helping us."*

Smoking and alcohol consumption

Children in re-ordered families were more likely to have tried cigarettes and to have drunk alcohol – precocious activities that some studies have linked by to an increased risk of subsequent involvement in serious problems such as drug taking, teenage sexual experience and criminality.[12] There were more children in re-ordered families who had "ever tried alcohol" than in intact families and they were also more likely to be current "drinkers".[13] Alcohol consumption was most common among children in the re-disrupted sub-group. There were eight instances of parents reporting occasions when their child had been very drunk, had drunk too much persistently, or had been in trouble because of activities related to alcohol – one in an intact family and seven in re-ordered families.

More children from re-ordered families said that their parents knew about their smoking and drinking and were more likely to report that they drank alcohol or smoked more freely at home. Children in intact families appeared to be more secretive about their activities. Only two children, both living in lone parent families, told the researchers that they had experimented with drugs.

Why parents thought their children were ill

"There have been no effects on her, I believe it all to be coincidence. She does bottle things up, but my son is very happy and doing well. They say he is university material."

Most parents of children who had experienced problems with their health said they did not know what caused their children's difficulties. However, more than half the parents in re-ordered families thought family change had affected their child's health, at least for a time and one in three related current problems directly to separation and divorce.

Nine children were described by their parents as having been badly affected at the time of separation and divorce, but were now reported to be "better". Seven out of ten non-resident parents in the study also thought their child's health had been affected at the time of separation and divorce – although half said their child was now "back to normal".

Information from GPs

Family doctors who returned questionnaires relating to the study children said they were much more likely to see parents rather than children from families affected by divorce, re-partnering and other changes. This finding appeared to indicate a lack of perception and knowledge about family circumstances on the part of GPs as twice as many study children from re-ordered families had visited their family doctor in the past 6 months compared with those in intact families.

In fact, like teachers (see below), doctors were not always sure of the children's family circumstances. In 40 cases the GP could not describe the family composition and a further 15 described it incorrectly. According to doctors there were also few differences between intact, lone, re-disrupted and step-families with regard to general or psychosomatic health problems. They had also observed little or no difference between different kinds of family group requiring frequent home visits or visiting their surgeries more than usual.

Few formal developmental problems were reported by GPs, although 20 per cent of children in re-ordered families were described as having hearing problems compared with 12 per cent of children in intact families. Other problems, including speech difficulties, were identified, but in very small numbers.

Education and schools

"When Dad left I just didn't want to go to school."

"Changes seemed not to have affected [her at] school. In fact the school say she is a model pupil."

After home, the school environment is where the child spends most time. The schools taking part in the study were wary about breaking confidentiality or were not always aware of the child's background. Previous research has found that knowledge of children's family circumstances can affect teachers' attitude to the pupil.[14]

Previous research has also emphasised the "re-enforcement" that schools can provide to help counteract the vulnerability that children display at times when there is conflict at home.[15] The present study is in accord with those findings. Nearly six out of ten children from re-ordered families said that teachers knew about their changed family circumstances and nearly a third had talked about it to their class teacher. Another one in five had discussed it with school friends.

Children in re-ordered families were slightly more likely to say that they were having general problems at school, but were much more likely to report having received extra help with school work. Receipt of that extra help should, in the authors' view, be interpreted as evidence of the positive way that schools can support children at a time of stress, rather than indicating that children from re-ordered families were, in any generalised sense, underachieving.[16]

School work

Children in the study were rather more likely than their parents to report problems with school work. They most often described difficulties with reading, with maths or with "just concentrating".

Figure 4.10 **Numbers of children reporting problems with their academic work at school**

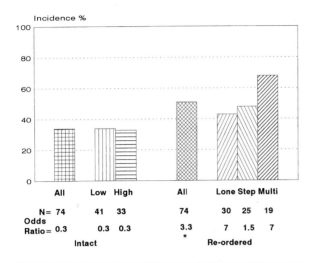

Figure 4.11 **Numbers of children who had received additional formal or informal support for their academic work**

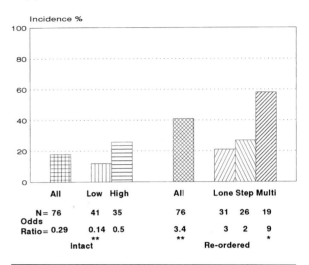

Those in re-ordered families reported more problems than children in intact families, and children in lone parent and step-families reported fewer problems than children in re-disrupted families (Figure 4.10). There was no difference between children from high- and low-conflict intact families. Children in re-ordered and intact families reported similar preferences for academic or practical subjects at school, although children and parents in re-ordered families reported more general problems with school work (see Appendix 3, Table 5).

Extra help

Children in low-conflict families were least likely to have received formal or informal additional help with school work, while those in re-disrupted families were much the most likely to have done so (Figure 4.11). There were two children from re-ordered families who had full-time helpers at school and a small group (8) were receiving special lessons. A number of parents were also working with teachers to give their children extra help (7 intact and 11 re-ordered).

Two of the children from re-disrupted families were described by their parents as having serious concentration problems, as was one child who had experienced prolonged "silent" conflict at a time when both parents were living in the same house awaiting divorce proceedings.

There were two children in intact families whose eating disorders were profoundly affecting their ability to cope in school, and three children from re-ordered families whose persistent and frequent refusal to attend school was clearly affecting their work.

Figure 4.12 **School changes additional to those imposed by school-age structures experienced by children (parents' data)**

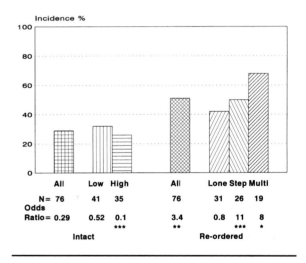

Changing schools

"I had to move schools because I kept jumping over the school fence and I lit a fire and threw stones. Mum tied my hands up when I did this."

About a third of all the children studied had changed schools for reasons other than those normally required by the local education authority between first, middle and high schools. Extra school changes were not always recognised as such by the child concerned, but whether measured by children's own reports or those of their parents, they had occurred more frequently among children in re-ordered families (Figure 4.12).

However, children in (first-time) lone parent families were not significantly more likely to have changed school than those in intact families. The measure also found that those living with parents in high-conflict marriages were, in this particular sample, least likely to have moved school.

Equal numbers of children in re-ordered and intact families reported that things were "better" after they had changed schools (six versus five). However, 13 children in re-ordered families, compared with eight children from intact families, reported that things were "worse". Ten per cent of children in re-ordered families compared with 5 per cent in intact families said that they had problems with friends after a school change which had created a feeling of isolation.

Problems with friends at school

More parents (66) said their children were having problems with friendships at school than the children (52) themselves said. But whereas the number of parents reporting children's difficulties was similar in re-ordered (35) and intact (31) families, children in re-ordered families (32) reported more problems than those in intact families (2). Problems with friends were an integral part of children's difficulties in coping with school. They were associated with changes of school and neighbourhood which, in some cases, had led to the child's not wanting to go to school. Children in re-ordered families were also more likely to say that their particular friends, like them, had parents who were separated or divorced. Seventy-five per cent had friends who had experienced separation and divorce, compared with 59 per cent of children in intact families.

Difficulties with teachers

By their own accounts and those of their parents, most children were " getting on well" at school and had few specific problems with teachers. Children were, however, more likely to report difficulties than their families (Figure 4.13).

Although children in re-ordered families reported slightly more problems with teachers than children in intact families, the difference was small and not statistically significant. There were no differences between sub-groups in either intact or re-ordered families (Figure 4.13). However, more children in re-ordered families (10) than intact families (4) said that teachers and other authority figures could sometimes upset them. Just a few children appeared to be in .

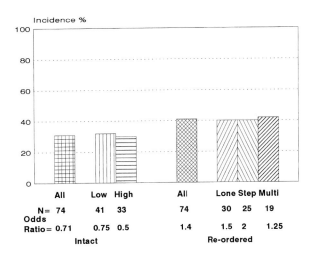

Figure 4.13 **Children's reports of difficulties with teachers at school**

continual conflict with a teacher and felt that they were being unfairly treated.

Truancy and school refusal

Among all the families in the study, 30 parents and 22 children mentioned problems with truancy or school refusal. Parents in re-ordered families were significantly more likely (20) to report such behaviour than intact families (10). Less seriously, but interestingly, there were 88 children who reported instances of "not wanting to go to school" – 40 came from intact families and 48 from re-ordered families. Particular problems with one teacher, or difficulties with pieces of unfinished homework were sometimes cited, while a few children said they had problems with friends that they did not want to face. A minority of children (12) in re-ordered families stated specifically that school was difficult for them when their parents separated; 15 parents reported acute problems for the child at school at the time of family breakdown. As one child put it *"Friends teased me at school and said I hadn't got a Dad. It was cruel."* Another told researchers *"The day Dad cut Mum's hand I couldn't concentrate – I didn't want to go to school."*

Information obtained from teachers

An incomplete response meant that the data collected from teachers was limited. Out of 90 school questionnaires returned, information was only available on 33 of the matched pairs. No clear picture of the schools' knowledge of different family groups emerged and, in some instances, they appeared unaware of family change. Schools, not improperly, felt that such matters should remain the "property" of the families concerned until they chose to share them. Some teachers also appeared wary of involvement with the research.[17] Assurances about parental consent for the school contact did not fully allay their fears; in the words of a teacher *"Schools are enormously vulnerable to angry parents."* As already suggested, other research has shown that teachers' responses and expectations of children can be affected by their knowledge of a child's family circumstances. As a result, they can have more negative expectations of children in re-ordered families; this did not seem to be the case in this study.[18]

Teachers perceived small, but not significant differences between children from re-ordered and intact families. The most striking finding was that teachers were less likely to identify problems than either the children's parents or the children themselves. Many, nevertheless, appeared supportive and concerned about the children, and showed awareness of the kinds of difficulties that children were under, including illnesses and rejection by peers.[19] They also indicated that some children who had faced difficulties at a time of family change were now making progress. They were aware of the more overt behaviour demonstrated by the children and could link this to family circumstances and events outside school.[20]

Social adjustment

When asked about future prospects for children, teachers anticipated slightly more problems with personal and social relationships for children from re-ordered families, compared with intact families.

Parental contact with school

Teachers reported that more parents from re-ordered families had "less contact" with the school than parents from intact families. Small numbers in both family groups were described as having "above average" contact. Lone parents were said to have the least contact – a finding which coincides with lone parents themselves saying they found it difficult to attend parents' evenings – lack of transport and baby-sitters being constraining factors.

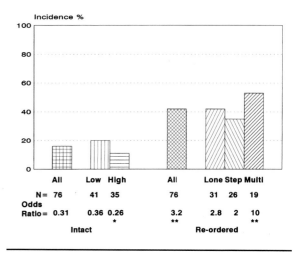

Figure 4.14 **Parents' views about whether their child's social life was restricted and unsatisfactory**

Social life

"I go out when I want to. I have total freedom."

Children were asked whether they felt that they had enough social contacts, if they had problems in making friends and how they got on with other children in general. They were also asked about bringing friends home (see Appendix 3, Table 6). Parents were questioned about their child's social life.[21]

Levels of dissatisfaction

Parents in re-ordered families were more often unhappy about their child's social life than those in intact families (Figure 4.14). The re-disrupted sub-group of families reported by far the most dissatisfaction.

Problems with friendships

All told, about a third of children felt they could have had more friends. Half said they had problems with friendships, with similar overall numbers occurring in both the re-ordered and intact families. Children in high-conflict intact families were more likely to say they had friendship problems than those in intact families where the levels of conflict were low. Children in re-disrupted and lone parent families were more likely to report difficulties than those living in step-families (Figure 4.15). However, none of the differences could be described as large.[22]

Many parents, but especially those in re-disrupted families, were likely to be worried about their children's friendships – particularly their choice of friends (Figure 4.16).

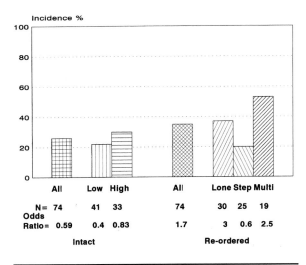

Figure 4.15 **Children who felt that they had problems with friendships**

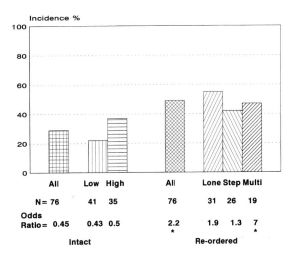

Figure 4.16 **Parents who were worried about their children's friendships**

Social isolation

Among re-ordered families, 19 parents reported that their children were socially isolated or anti-social, compared with three in intact families. Seven out of eight children who said they had no friends came from re-ordered families. Of those who reported that they found it hard to make friends, the highest proportion lived in re-disrupted families (ten out of 19). Parents in re-ordered families were also more likely to believe that family problems had interfered with their child's social life, (11) compared with those in intact families (five).

Choice of friends

Most children in both family groups socialised children from their own age group. However, more children in re-ordered families (27) said they could bring home friends without prior warning than those in intact families (16).

Friends who have been in trouble with the law

Twenty per cent of children from intact families, and 28 per cent from re-ordered families, reported having friends who had been in trouble with the law – a figure that included nearly half of the children in "re-disrupted" families. Very few children in the study had themselves been involved in any criminal activity, apart from one incident of rowdy behaviour following too much alcohol at a party that got out of control, and another where the police were called following a cycle ride on private property.

Parental supervision

Almost all parents of children in both the age groups under study claimed to know where their children were (casual and organised socialising) while they were pursuing their social lives. Only five parents said that they had a problem "keeping track" of their children.

Non-resident parents

Although non-resident parents knew less about their child's social life than the resident parent, a minority were involved to the extent of being aware of their child's choice of friends and welcoming them as visitors. Even so, most non-resident parents and their children saw their contact arrangements as exclusively "family" time, of which friends were not a part.

Mood and behaviour

"I'm not sure how much she's upset by what has happened, and how much is normal teenage behaviour."

Parents in re-ordered families (44) were more likely to say that their child's mood had become less equable since divorce than parents of intact families (who were asked about "recent" behaviour (27)), but the differences were not particularly large (Figure 4.17).[23]

Among the re-ordered families, parents in (first-time) step-families were most likely to report mood problems. High-conflict families were slightly more like re-ordered families, and only slightly more likely to report a change.

Figure 4.17 **Negative changes in child's mood reported by parents**

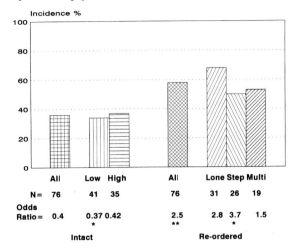

Incidence %

	All	Low	High	All	Lone	Step	Multi
N=	76	41	35	76	31	26	19
Odds Ratio=	0.4	0.37*	0.42	2.5**	2.8	3.7*	1.5

Intact   Re-ordered

Figure 4.19 **Numbers of parents who said that their child's behaviour was upsetting to them**

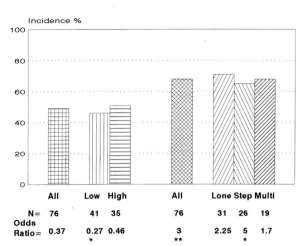

Incidence %

	All	Low	High	All	Lone	Step	Multi
N=	76	41	35	76	31	26	19
Odds Ratio=	0.37	0.27*	0.46	3**	2.25	5*	1.7

Intact   Re-ordered

Parents in both family groups agreed that age-related changes, change of school, the influence of "unsuitable friends", or friends of the opposite sex, could have been the catalyst for negative mood changes. A number of children in re-ordered families were also reported to be difficult to manage when they returned from visiting their non-resident parent.[24] Some were said to be withdrawn and sad, others truculent and argumentative. *"He's often difficult the evening he comes back from seeing his father. The longer he stays the more upset he is."* (see Appendix 3. Table 7).

Behaviour – the view of parents

Parents in re-ordered families, especially lone parents, were more likely to express concern

Figure 4.18 **Numbers of parents concerned about their child's behaviour**

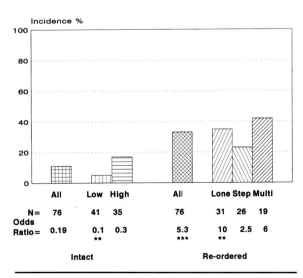

Incidence %

	All	Low	High	All	Lone	Step	Multi
N=	76	41	35	76	31	26	19
Odds Ratio=	0.19	0.1**	0.3	5.3***	10**	2.5	6

Intact   Re-ordered

about their children's current behaviour than those whose families remained intact. They were more likely to say that the child had become hard to manage or was exhibiting serious behaviour problems, especially just after their parents' separation (Figure 4.18).

Parents in re-ordered families were also significantly more likely to report that their child's behaviour upset them (Figure 4.19). Step-parents were most likely to be upset compared with their matched pairs in intact families. Twenty-four children (17 in re-ordered families, seven in intact families) either showed signs of developing serious behaviour problems or had blatant manifestations of disturbance. *"He throws things at the wall and writes on the wall, and I'm afraid to stop him."*

Both resident and non-resident parents in re-ordered families, meanwhile, acknowledged that family breakdown had contributed to their child's unhappiness and, in some cases, to "changed behaviour". *"She was very quiet for a while and often wasn't very well."* Unhappiness continued to be associated with times when visiting arrangements meant children moved between their resident and non-resident parents. Even so, the behaviour of a minority of children (12) was said to have improved following their parents' separation.[25]

Behaviour – children's own views

Children's views were sought about their own behaviour towards others and towards authority. They were also asked how they felt about the way others treated them.

The Exeter Family Study

Figure 4.20 **Numbers of children who thought that their behaviour was upsetting for other people**

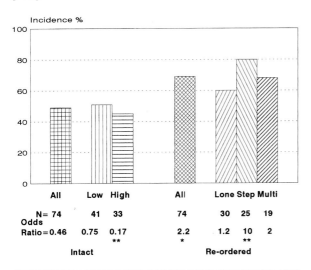

Figure 4.21 **Numbers of children who had significant arguments with resident parent(s)**

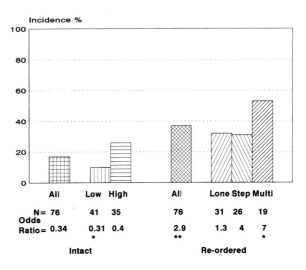

Six out of ten children acknowledged that their own behaviour might be upsetting for other people, but this was more frequently the case among children in re-ordered families (Figure 4.20). Children variously described themselves as awkward, rude, argumentative or annoying, fighting with their brothers and sisters and causing problems for their parents. Those living in step-families were most likely to report that their behaviour upset other people compared with their matched pairs in intact families. Children living in intact families where their parents were in conflict were less likely to report upsetting behaviour of their own (a finding that contrasts somewhat with the views of their parents recorded in Figure 4.19) .

Nearly twice as many children in re-ordered families complained that the behaviour of other family members was upsetting to them (31) than those from intact families (17). Some spoke of "interfering" and "irritating" grannies or of brothers and sisters being difficult. Sibling rivalry appeared to be serious in one or two cases.

Relationships between children and parents

This section looks at the disagreements between children and their parents, children's awareness of and reaction to family rows, discussions about personal relationships and number of family outings. Generally speaking, it shows that parents in re-ordered families reported more disagreements with their children than those in intact families, but that children in *both* types of family reported similar numbers of problems.[26]

Arguments with parents

Overall, parents in re-ordered families reported more major disagreements with their children than those in intact families (Figure 4.21). Intact families where the parents were themselves in conflict were closer (marginally) to lone and step parents on this measure than those where conflict levels were low. Among re-ordered families, parents in re-disrupted families were most likely to report problems. Previous research has suggested that children respond to changing parental situations on a very immediate level, which can be reflected in the number and kinds of arguments between parents and children.[27]

A small number of children reported arguing with their mothers about money, appearances and friends, as well as their fighting with brothers and sisters and "not wanting to help around the house". Major rows with mothers were most often reported by children in re-disrupted families. Children in re-ordered families were less likely than their parents to report rows with the father figure in the household.

"I don't know Dad well enough to argue with him."

It was noticeable that children in re-ordered families reported very few rows with their non-resident parent. One non-resident mother suggested that because her child spent so little time with her she avoided arguments and tended to "give in" to unreasonable demands: *"She pushes for more money, more outings, more attention all the time she is with me"*. While some

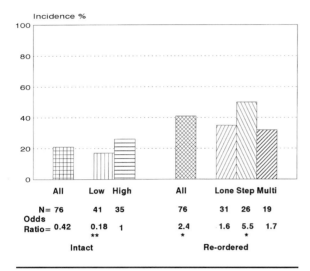

	All	Low	High	All	Lone	Step	Multi
N=	76	41	35	76	31	26	19
Odds Ratio=	0.42	0.18 **	1	2.4 *	1.6	5.5 *	1.7

Intact   Re-ordered

non-resident parents did report arguments with their children, resident parents and step-parents, by contrast, felt that they had the major disciplinary role, and, consequently, expected more arguments (see Appendix 3, Table 8).[28]

Parental Expectations

Closely linked to arguments between parents and children were reported problems about parental expectations of their children. Parents in re-ordered families and high-conflict intact families were more likely to agree that they had harboured unreasonable or excessively high expectations of their children (Figure 4.22). Step-parents were especially likely to describe their expectations as too high compared to their matched pair. Some parents in re-ordered families explained this as wanting their child to "grow up and be responsible" after divorce, shouldering a greater share of organisation in the family: *"The facts were they had to do more things for themselves"*. This sense of unreasonable expectations appeared to be confined to resident parents in the study. Non-resident parents felt they did not expect too much, but one in four accused their former spouse of doing so: *"He was upset and stressed, his mother used him as a shield"*. Non-resident parents felt they did not (or could not) expect too much because their relationship with their children was too tenuous.

Rules and discipline

Although intact families reported more emphasis on "formal" rules in their homes than re-ordered families, it became clear that there were differences in the kinds of behaviour that the two types of family were seeking to control. Rules about tidiness and helping in the house were more likely to be reported by intact families, whereas rules about swearing, rudeness and unhelpfulness were considered more important by re-ordered families. Rules about bedtime, meals, manners, sibling rows and general boundaries such as "knowing where the children are" were equally important to both family groups. The one area in which children's perceptions of the importance of house rules varied from that of their parents was over not fighting with their siblings, which children regarded as a major contributor to family harmony.

Re-ordered families were more likely to say that they needed to discipline their children (75 per cent) compared to intact families (50 per cent), and that they disciplined their children frequently (every day, or two to three times a week). Most children in both family groups said their parents used discipline in a planned way, tending to ground them, stop pocket money, deny sweets, ban television, or send them to their bedrooms, rather than shout at them or physically punish them. Similar numbers of children in the intact (13) and re-ordered families (15) reported that they were smacked and that their parents shouted at them (35 in intact families; 42 in re-ordered families). Parents' accounts of disciplinary measures were in most respects similar to those of their children, but fewer admitted to using "smacking". One child said that there were no punishments in their house *"because my Mum expects good behaviour and gets it!"*.

Family outings

Fewer family visits and "get togethers" were reported by re-ordered families, and they were less likely to go on family outings than intact families (it was, however, apparent that children in the older age group were generally less likely to take part in family activities because of increasing involvement in peer-group activities). Re-disrupted and lone parent families reported fewer family outings than step-families (Figure 4.23).

Figure 4.23 **Numbers of parents who said that they had no regular family outings**

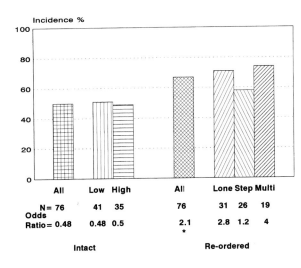

Both parents and children in re-ordered families ascribed less frequent family outings to the effects of separation and divorce and the division of the child's time between parents. Parents as well as children said they missed this aspect of family life. Parents also frequently described "missing" their children when they were with their other parent. *"They have nice times without me"*. A few, however, also said they enjoyed the freedom of time on their own: *"I hadn't realised the bonus of having time off without the children"* (see Appendix 3, Table 8). Of the non-resident parents who were interviewed, 37 per cent said that they still had "family-type" outings with their children and tried to make contact visits as normal as possible.

Parental Rows

"I can remember one argument when Dad shot the cat."

Fewer than one in seven children in re-ordered families were unable to remember difficulties between their parents at the time of separation and divorce. They were significantly more likely to recall "serious" rows between their parents than children whose families remained intact. Conversely, a higher proportion of parents in intact families (7) said that they never disagreed in front of the children, compared with re-ordered families (17), who felt that they had been less able to hide the conflict from their children.

Nearly half the children in re-ordered families (47 per cent) compared with less than a quarter (23 per cent) in intact families said that they "kept

out of the way when their parents argued", although they were well aware of the disagreement. Five children in intact families said that they joined in when their parents argued: *"I stay awake until they go to sleep in case they have arguments and then I try and stop them. So far I have succeeded, but I don't want Dad to leave again"*. (10-year-old whose parents divorced but are now together again). Three children in each family group were "not keen" to discuss the matter.

Domestic Violence

Physical violence was described by one or other partner in a quarter of re-ordered families (20) but in only two intact families. Its occurrence was known to three out of four children in the families where it was reported. Some parents said they shut children in the bedroom to protect them, while children described putting their heads under pillows, walking out of the house and going to grandparents, and, in three cases, intervening to protect their mother: *"I used to sit on the stairs every morning early and wait, because that's when the trouble started before he went to work"*.

Personal Relationships

Children were less likely than their parents to say that they confided in their parents about personal problems. Children from intact families reported less discussion of personal issues than those in re-ordered families, possibly because they felt they had less to discuss. Children in re-ordered families were more likely to discuss personal issues with their resident, rather than their non-resident, parent. Indeed, a few non-resident fathers who were living with new partners believed their children were more likely to seek advice and support from their step-parent than from them.

Fewer than four out of ten children reported having a current friend of the opposite sex or having had one in the past, although having a boy or girlfriend was more common among the 13- and 14-year-olds. Those from re-ordered families were also more likely to have a friend of the opposite sex than those from intact families. Most contact with friends of the opposite sex, for both age groups, was through school or outside the home, though a minority brought their girl-or boyfriends home. A minority of parents in both intact and re-ordered families were worried about their children's relationships with the opposite sex, something of which their children were aware.

Contact with relatives

Parents and children were asked about the frequency of contact with relatives and their importance to the child. They were asked to say which relatives provided them with help and support. Children were questioned about changes in contact with grandparents and whether they wished for more. Those in re-ordered families were asked about contact with the parents of their resident and non-resident parent, and this was compared with the contact that children in intact families had with their maternal or paternal grandparents. In all but seven re-ordered families, the children's resident parent was their mother, so any element of discrepancy in the analyses in this section is slight[29].

Re-ordered families tended, in any case, to see more of their mother's relatives, to the extent that even three of the six children who lived with their fathers still had good contact with maternal grandparents. Three-quarters of re-ordered families reported less contact with paternal grandparents following divorce, although the remaining group of grandparents made an effort to keep in touch with the child. Seventeen remarried families reported good support from new relationship grandparents. Overall, a third of children in re-ordered families had contact with additional sets of "grandparents" as a result of their parents forming new relationships. A minority (9) also lost touch with them following multiple disruption. While parents reported that new "grandparents" were supportive and included the children in the family, other research has shown that these relationships may not be long lasting, and, as with the non-resident parent grandparents, children were more likely to lose touch with these new relatives following multiple disruption[30].

Patterns of contact

Among intact families it was evident that patterns of contact with grandparents had altered over time. Changes were age-related as children developed their own interests, or because families had moved away from grandparents. For a small number of intact families (6) there was little contact with relatives, and relationships with them were poor. This appeared to have been the case throughout the children's lives (see Appendix 3, Table 9). In the case of re-ordered families, however, three times as many children said they had reduced contact with grandparents.

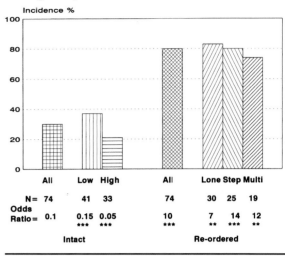

Figure 4.24 **Children's view of reduced contact with grandparents**

Children in lone, step, and re-disrupted families were all significantly more likely to report seeing their grandparents less often (Figure 4.24). Among these families, a number of different contact patterns were identified:

- Children's contact with grandparents had remained the same despite separation or divorce.

- Contact with maternal grandparents had remained strong and in some cases increased after parental separation.

- Children had remained in contact with paternal and maternal relatives, but one or other parent was "excluded" when meetings took place.

- Children saw more of the non-resident parent's grandparents (usually paternal) because contact visits took place at the grandparents' home.

- Children had lost touch with one set of grandparents altogether.

- The resident parent had kept in touch with both sets of grandparents "for the sake of the children", usually by telephone or post. Children, however, still made separate visits with one or other parent.

Children often said they found it difficult and stressful to visit grandparents when one or other parent was excluded. Parents also found such situations painful. Children's Christmases were often divided between separate visits to warring sets of relatives, or else they were expected to visit different sides of the family in alternate years. The evidence of the study was that children found visiting grandparents separately or with just one

Figure 4.25 **Numbers of parents reporting contact with resident parent/maternal grandparents as monthly or less**

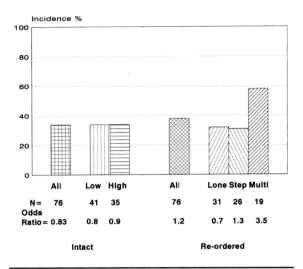

Incidence %

	All	Low	High	All	Lone	Step	Multi
N=	76	41	35	76	31	26	19
Odds Ratio=	0.83	0.8	0.9	1.2	0.7	1.3	3.5

Intact   Re-ordered

of their parents more distressing even than losing contact with them altogether. Children were also upset if a parent's new partner clearly disapproved of their grandparents: *"Mum's boyfriend didn't like me, but he specially didn't like me when I was like my Gran. He used to say shut up, you sound just like your Gran".*

Contact with maternal grandparents

Out of 152 families in the study, 97 reported having contact more than once a month with maternal (or resident parent) grandparents. Intact families reported almost the same level of contact as re-ordered families. There was also little

Figure 4.26 **Numbers of parents reporting contact with non-resident parent/paternal grandparents as monthly or less**

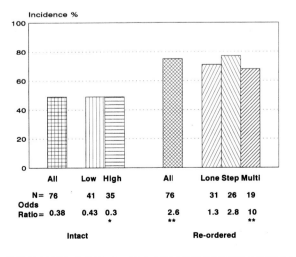

Incidence %

	All	Low	High	All	Lone	Step	Multi
N=	76	41	35	76	31	26	19
Odds Ratio=	0.38	0.43	0.3 *	2.6 **	1.3	2.8	10 **

Intact   Re-ordered

difference between re-ordered (29) and intact (26) families, who had infrequent contact, seeing them monthly or less (Figure 4.25). However, the re-disrupted sub-group reported less contact than other re-ordered groups and by comparison with their matched pairs in intact families.

Contact with paternal grandparents

All family groups in the study had less contact with paternal (or non-resident parent) grandparents than they did with maternal grandparents. Sixty families reported more than monthly contact compared with 92 families who reported less. Re-ordered families (55) were significantly more likely to have infrequent contact with paternal (or non-resident parent) grandparents than intact families (37). Children in re-disrupted families, again, had the least contact compared with other re-ordered families and their intact family matched pair (Figure 4.26).

This finding made it all the more noticeable that those children in the study who said they wished they could see their paternal grandparents more often were almost entirely confined to intact families. Although children in re-ordered families had less contact with paternal (non-resident parent) grandparents, and were said to receive less support, they did not report wanting to see them more often.

Christmas and other holidays

Re-ordered families described how contact with grandparents had altered for major events such as Christmas, Easter, birthdays and holidays. When their parents were still living together, the majority (47) had seen both maternal and paternal grandparents at Christmas, while only three had only seen their maternal grandparents. Now, however, just under half (34) were seeing only maternal grandparents at Christmas.
It was also found that twice as many children in re-ordered families (14) as in intact families (7) had no contact with grandparents at Christmas, either now or in the past. Among intact families, meanwhile, the vast majority (65) reported seeing both sets of grandparents.

Support from grandparents

In both intact and re-ordered families maternal (resident parent) grandparents were generally felt to be more supportive of both parents and children in the study (Figures 4.27 and 4.28).

Figure 4.27 **Perceived lack of support for child by resident parent/maternal grandparents**

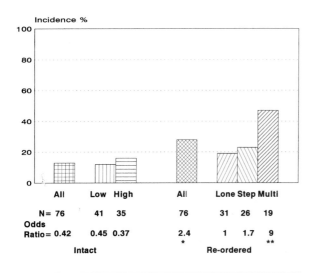

Figure 4.29 **Number of families where non-resident parent/paternal grandparents were seen as unsupportive to child**

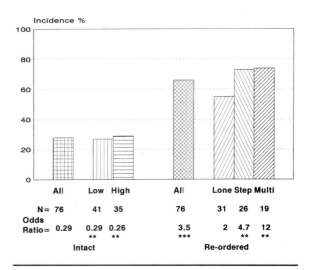

Figure 4.28 **Resident parent's view of own parents/maternal grandparents being unsupportive of themselves**

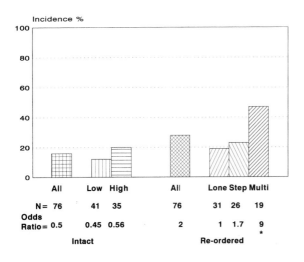

families were significantly more likely to say this.

The impression given by some parents in re-ordered families was that grandparents who were unsupportive were also more likely to oppose their children's efforts to re-build a social life or find a new partner. "*After I left [my husband] my Dad wouldn't speak to me he thought I should have stayed'. He said: "A good hiding never did no one no harm".*

Discussion

The study measured outcomes for children by using parent, child and professional reports of well-being, problems and needs in five main areas of children's lives: health, education, social life, mood and behaviour.[31] Children's self-esteem was also measured by a self-completed Rosenberg scale.[32]

Parents' and childrens' perceptions

Replies to parts of the questionnaire seeking information about factual events revealed high levels of agreement between the children and their parents. In contrast, the professionals, whether teachers or doctors, often had incomplete and inaccurate information about the type of family where the child was living, particularly when multiple disruption had taken place. Teachers were less likely than parents to acknowledge that particular children had special needs, and doctors did not always recognise the occasions when children presented psycho-somatic symptoms.[33] In most areas there was close agreement between individual children's

A lack of support was more frequently reported by re-ordered families than intact families. It was found, however, that this difference was almost entirely attributable to the re-disrupted family group. Children and parents who had experienced multiple family disruption were significantly less likely to receive support from maternal grandparents.

A somewhat different picture emerged in respect of support received from paternal (non-resident parent) grandparents.

Significantly, two-thirds of re-ordered families reported a lack of support compared with a third of intact families (Figure 4.29). Similar proportions of step- and re-disrupted families said paternal grandparents were unsupportive, but compared with their intact family controls, re-disrupted perceptions of difficulties and those of their parents, although non-resident parents more often showed a lack of detailed knowledge (which they associated with their feelings of loss). In some areas, such as the number and type of psychosomatic symptoms, or problems with friends at school, the children reported more difficulties than their parents. In other areas, such as appropriateness of friends and problems with social life, parents had more concerns than their children.

Intact and re-ordered families

Children and their parents in re-ordered families more often reported difficulties in each of the five areas under study than those in intact families. They were more likely to have encountered health problems (especially psychosomatic disorders), to have needed extra help at school, to have experienced friendship difficulties and to suffer from low self-esteem. These differences were highly significant, whether the comparisons were for individual questions or areas, for total scores in each area or for aggregate scores across all five. Statistically, the odds ratios from comparing matched pairs were mostly from two- to six-fold, and were never below unity. Multivariate analysis confirmed that living in a re-ordered family, as opposed to an intact family, was the most significant association with poorer outcomes for the children.

Self-esteem

From the Rosenberg scale and other measurements of well-being it was clear the children who had experienced their parents' separation and divorce had poorer self-esteem and lower estimates of self-worth than those whose families had remained intact.

Lowered self-esteem was also related to the difficulties that were examined in other areas of children's lives. Those reporting a reduced sense of their own worth were more likely to report health problems, or to have been referred for psychological or psychiatric assistance. They were also more likely to have needed extra help with school work, to have encountered friendship problems, and to describe themselves as generally "unhappy". In the mutivariate analyses, child scores for self-image were the variables most closely linked to other outcome scores, whether the data was from the parent's or child's perspective, and regardless of family sub-group. This finding is consistent with previous studies,

where low self-esteem has been identified as a key indicator of problems in other areas of children's lives.[34]

Lone, step and re-disrupted families

In spite of the very considerable differences in economic and social well-being between the lone and step-parent families in the study (see Chapter 3), there were few marked differences in the measured outcomes for children. Yet the outcomes for children in re-disrupted families were much less likely to be satisfactory, although they were no worse off financially than the (first-time) lone parent group. In addition to problems with their health and schooling, children in re-disrupted families were more likely to describe themselves as "often unhappy" or "miserable". Multivariate analysis of either the whole group or of the two main groups separately failed to reveal any significant associations between financial hardship and poor outcomes for the children. This finding contrasts with the results from some longitudinal studies.[35]

The findings are, however, in accord with American studies suggesting that outcomes for children whose families have gone through multiple disruption are often significantly poorer than for (first-time) lone parent or step-families.[36] Multivariate analysis in the current study confirmed this association in both the total scores, and the number of areas affected. However, the effect was, stronger in the child's, rather than parent's, perception of problems. This suggests that parents who have undergone more than one change of partner may be more likely to under-estimate, or fail to recognise, the problems that their children may face.[37]

Conflict

Conflict between parents has been associated in other research with low self-image in children[38] and with many of the poor outcomes for children that have been described among those who experience divorce.[39] Some studies suggest that if parents in intact families are in continuous conflict, this may be more damaging for the children than divorce itself.[40]

Rows in the present study were recalled by 75 per cent of children who were living with both biological parents, and in 97 per cent of families where children had experienced separation and divorce (and were old enough to remember).

However, rows recalled by the child as "more serious" than silence or shouting were significantly more frequent in the re-ordered families: 31 per cent compared with 11 per cent in intact families.

Where children were living in intact families marked by discord between their parents, the outcomes for self-esteem, psychological health and social well-being were intermediate between those of children in re-ordered families and intact families where the level of reported conflict was low. However, in this study, the outcomes more closely resembled those for children in other, intact families than those in re-ordered families. The study also found there were quite marked differences in self-esteem between children in re-ordered families according to whether conflict between their parents had continued after the divorce, and whether the children, themselves, were especially unhappy with the contact arrangements.[41]

Domestic violence

Actual violence was recalled by one or other partner in 20 re-ordered families and in two intact families. Seven out of the 20 who had experienced physical violence had also been through more than two marital disruptions. Multivariate analysis showed that when the type of family in which children were living was taken into account, the association between marital violence and their poor outcomes ceased to be significant. However, although re-ordered families are likely to recall the existence of domestic violence that contributed to the breakdown of the parental relationship, its presence in intact families may be under-reported. All the children in re-ordered families who could remember violence between their parents were very pleased to have been removed from that relationship, but, conversely, they still expressed confused feelings of missing their absent fathers. Not all had been subjected to violence themselves, and even those who had, appeared to combine anger with concern.

Effects of family breakdown

On average, poorer outcomes were reported by study children whose parents had separated than by those whose parents were living together. Moreover, the outcomes for children in "high conflict" intact families, more closely resembled those for children in "low conflict" intact families than those in re-ordered families. Conflict and violence had been much more frequent in the pre-divorce relationships of parents now living in re-ordered families. But it was also clear that these had often been made worse, or even begun, at the time when one or other partner decided to separate.[42]

Thus, while the previously recognised adverse effects of parental conflict and financial hardship on children are supported by this study, it seems that family breakdown leading to the loss of a parent from the home itself exerts an even greater influence over the outcomes. This finding accords with analysis of some[43] longitudinal British and American studies monitoring children over time, and qualitative studies such as those carried out by Wallerstein et al and Mitchell,[44] but is at variance with others.[45] The assumption is that parental conflict will cease following divorce, but for some families divorce instigates conflict which will continue into the post-divorce period.[46] Separation, when the child becomes a member of a one parent family may be welcomed by the resident parent as release from the empty shell of a failed relationship. But for the child, the loss of one parent, while accepted superficially, can be more ambivalent and complex in the long term,[47] even after a violent marriage.

Outcomes for children after the lone parents' subsequent re-partnering do not, for the most part, appear to be significantly worse, while their socio-economic status and sense of well-being are actually seen to improve. The major exceptions to this finding concern mood and behaviour. Meanwhile, the loss of a second parent figure, what the present study describes as "re-disruption", seems to be associated with much poorer outcomes for the child.

Expectations and the future

"He'll have to work hard not to turn out like his father."

Parents' expectations for the future were described in a more negative way than the child's own view. Over half the parents in both intact and re-ordered families reported that they were uncertain about the future for the family, whereas they were more positive about their children's future, 32 intact compared with 24 re-ordered families reporting uncertainty. Fears reported by parents included poor expectations of employment, lack of confidence in the child to apply him/herself and fear of the child repeating mistakes made by the parent.

The Exeter Family Study

One mother, who had married at 16, and had experienced two marital breakdowns said *"I have a dream that when the kids grow up they will have good jobs and a house, etc. They'll be more of a family than I am with mine."* Another expressed her concern for her daughter's future *"She wants babies, I hope she won't enter into a relationship before she's ready. Like me, she's attracted to lame ducks."* Conversely other parents and children reported that *"I see no reason why things won't work out"*.

Though re-ordered families slightly more often reported pessimism about the future for their child, particularly in re-disrupted families, the differences were not marked and odds ratios suggest only a 1.5 to 2 fold relative risk.

Children's own view of future expectations about marriage and children was similar in both re-ordered and intact families. In spite of the children's different experiences of "family", most children were positive about having their own children in the future, though one child was very clear about her intentions *"I won't get married because I don't like boys!"*. Children in intact families were slightly more likely to report that they did not want to have children of their own when they were older (see Appendix 3, Table 10).[48]

Case histories: the effects of time

For two out of three of the study children living in re-ordered families, the separation and/or divorce of their biological parents was an event that had occurred four or more years before the interview (Table 4.1).

Table 4.1 **Re-ordered families in the Exeter Study: time elapsed since separation/ divorce**

5 or more years	34
4 to 5 years	32
Less than 4 years	5
Less than 1 year	5

The numbers in the present study were small, making it difficult to reach broad conclusions as to the effects of time on children's reactions to change and their adaptation to separation and divorce. However, as in previous research[49], it would appear that children who have experienced conflict leading to family breakdown identify three distinct phases:

1. *An acute stage* for which children are not generally well prepared.[50] Parents in the Exeter study often acknowledged that their children had received little by way of initial explanation for the departure of one parent from the home: *"He told them he was going on holiday he never came back"*. Some parents described their children in the first year after divorce as having become very quiet, withdrawn or exhibiting very disturbed behaviour.

2. *A middle stage* when life for some children becomes more stable as they adapt to altered family patterns.[51] Others, however, are deeply affected by changes of house, school and socio-economic status, as well as unsatisfactory contact arrangements. In the study, they indicated that their lives had improved once parents were able to talk to each other and regular contact had been established with their non-resident parent: *"Things were bad but are now better"*. Children who were at this middle stage, either reported improvements or were still experiencing difficulties at school or with friends. In many instances they seemed unaware of their own withdrawn approach to life. *"I don't like seeing Dad with his new family, but I've got used to it"*.

3. *Long-term* In circumstances where the acute and middle stages persist, problems can amalgamate into long-term psychological difficulties and continuing problems concerning health, school-work and unresolved conflict with the non-resident parent.[52] In situations where parents do not speak to each other and no exanplations have ever been given to the child, it may be particularly difficult for the child to come to terms with his/her parents' separation. In the study, a further family transition at this stage added to the unresolved first situation, sometimes compounded the child's confusion and difficulties: *"I shan't mind as much if John leaves Mum this time, it won't be like when Dad left."*

Time on its own did not seem to be the most important influence on the outcomes for children, and clearly much depended on what else was happening in the their lives. For example, children in intact families reported changes associated with growing-up, such as less contact with grandparents, fewer family outings and a reduction in the amount of time that parents and children spent together. Children in re-ordered families had experienced these changes too, but there were added complications. Most obviously, they were likely to have less contact with one (non-resident) parent and to have spent more time with their resident parent as a direct result of separation and divorce.

The case histories opposite draw together some of the threads described in this chapter, as woven into the lives of different children in the study in the period following their parents' separation and divorce.

Case histories: the effects of time

Jack (aged 10)

Jack's mother was 17 and his father was 18 when he was born. He has no memory of the latter. Towards the end of the first year of his life, his father went abroad and has not returned. Jack lived with his mother and her parents until he was 3 years old; he then lived alone with his mother until she remarried when he was six and the family moved into its present home with Jack's stepfather.

Two years later, Jack's half-brother was born and was discovered to have severe mental and physical handicaps. His mother has found caring for this child very time-consuming and is sometimes tired and unwell. Jack has reacted by insisting that he is ill, absenteeism from school, and by being unable to concentrate when he is there.

Jack's mother had asked his stepfather to leave the home just before the family was interviewed, as their relationship had deteriorated. The step-father still refuses to accept this and frequently returns. Both Jack and his mother are frightened of his bullying behaviour and Jack admits to not knowing how to react.

Jack's paternal grandparents have recently made contact, asking to see him. His father has meanwhile, begun to write to both him and mother. He has been sending money and presents, and has asked to see Jack when he returns to the country in 6 months time. Both mother and child are confused by this new development in their lives.

Tom (aged 12)

A year ago Tom's mother left his father after a 12-year relationship during which she had been repeatedly physically abused. Tom cannot remember a time when domestic violence did not occur and he saw his role, from a very early age, as trying to protect his mother. She finally decided that she was not prepared to live with the situation any longer, and took Tom and his sister to friends. The family has since moved twice into temporary accommodation. Tom and his sister have remained at the same schools and have weekly contact with their father, which they find stressful. Tom's sister appears acutely distressed by the family changes.

Both mother and child say that they have found life much better during the past year, since they left the family home. There is a sense of relief and Tom says that he sleeps well (which he did not do before) and that his fears for his mother's safety have disappeared. He is also doing well at school.

Joe (aged 10)

Joe's father has just left the family home and divorce proceedings are in progress. His father had wanted to end the marriage some time ago, but financial and employment constraints meant that the parents had stayed in the same house, with communication between them broken down. Joe's acute psychological and emotional distress in response to this was made worse by his father's eventual departure.

The parents have decided to sell the family home and Joe and his mother are about to move to a new town (to be near maternal grandparents). Ahead of him, therefore, lies a change of home, school and friends.

Joe sees his father frequently and he is often withdrawn and weepy for a day or two after returning to his mother. His parents still find it very difficult to communicate.

Peter (aged 14)

Peter's parents separated when he was five. During the next two years he and his sister had limited contact with their father. This eventually ceased and there has been no contact for the past seven years. Peter, his mother and sister moved to their present home at the time of marital breakdown, so that his school and home have remained stable for many years.

His mother has not formed a new permanent relationship since the end of her first marriage and has tried to keep life as constant as possible for the children. She has a part time job, so that she can be at home during school holidays and after school. There have been financial constraints which Peter's mother feels strongly about as the children's father is very wealthy.

Peter feels ambivalent towards his father. He says he has come to terms with the fact that his father does not contact him, and does not wish to see him. But he says he may make contact with his father in the future. Peter is doing well at school, has a good social life, and hopes to go on to university.

1   Such as might be experienced by up to 30 per cent of the children in the study overall.

2   Rutter, M. (1989) Resilience in the face of adversity: Protective factors and resistance to psychiatric disorders. *British Journal of Psychiatry* **147**, 598–611.

3   Wadsworth, M. (1991) The *Imprint of Time. Childhood History and Adult Life.* Clarendon Press.

4   See also Santrock, J., Warshak, R., Lindberg, C. & Meadows, L. (1982).

5   Wallerstein, J & Kelly, J. (1980); Peterson, J. & Zill, J. (1986).

6   Resident parents in this study, as in others, were also found to be unaware of their children's true feelings of non-well-being at the time of divorce because of their own stress.

7   Rosenberg, J. (1979).

8   These findings agree with some studies that found that lowered self-esteem was more common in re-ordered families (Peterson, J. & Zill, N. 1986); other studies link levels of self-esteem to the child's relationship with their resident and non-resident parent (Parish, T. et al. 1980).

9   Wadsworth, M. (1991).

10 The longitudinal studies (Wadsworth, M. 1986 et al.; Hetherington, E.M. 1986) also report an increased risk of children with psychosomatic health problems in re-ordered families. See also Chester, R. (1973); Dominian (1991).

11 See also Douglas, J. (1970, 1973); Wadsworth, M. et al. (1986).

12 Phinney, V.G., Jensen, L.C., Olsen, J.A. & Cundick, B. (1990).

13 Utting, D. (1993) Crime *and the Family.* Family Policies Study Centre.

14 Touliatos, J. & Lindholm, B. (1980). See also Ferri, E. (1976).

15 Rutter, M. (1989); Jenkins, J. & Smith, M. (1990).

16 Jenkins, J. & Smith, M. (1991).

17 See Hodges, W.F. (1986); a review of research and school interventions to support children who have experienced divorce.

18 Touliatos, J. & Lindholm, B. (1980). See also Ferri, E. (1976).

19 See also Hodges, W.F. (1986).

20 Touliatos, J. & Lindholm, B. (1990) and Ferri, E. (1976), whose studies found that knowledge of children's family status affected teachers' responses to children.

21 See Wallerstein, J. & Kelly, J. (1980); Hodges, W. (1986).

22 Elliot, J. & Richards, M. (1991); Wallerstein, J. & Kelly, J. (1974) discuss the effects of separation and divorce on the child's social networks.

23 See Schaffer, H. (1990), who reports that childrens' behaviour can contribute to the parental response particulary after divorce which then in turn influences the child. See also Capaldi, D. (1989).

24 The longitudinal studies show that children mostly settle down over time following separation and divorce (Hetherington, E.M. et al. (1992) but continuing conflict concerning contact can adversely affect childrens' behaviour. See also Touliatos, J. & Lindholm, B. 1980).

25 Hetherington, E.M. & Cox, M. (1986). This paper discusses the child's improved responses in some situations to divorce when the everyday conflict between their parents is less immediate.

26 Other studies have found that children's behaviour is related to the mood and response of parents to the child. In Hetherington, E.M. et al (1986) parents under most stress are less tolerant of their child's vagaries.

27 Schaffer, H.R. (1990) Making Decisions about Children; Psychological Questions and Answers. Blackwell. See also Hetherington E.M., Cox, M. & Cox, R.(1985).

28 See discussion in Hodges, W.F. (1986) and a study by Pasley et al (1987) which found that in some cases resident parents had the main share of responsibility for discipline etc. while the non-resident parents role was almost peripheral.

29 It should also be noted that more maternal (123) than paternal (96) grandparents lived locally which affected contact partterns for both intact families and for re-ordered families.

30 See Willmott, P. (1986) and Finch, J. (1993) studies which explore the importance of cross-generational networks and the mutual advantage to both parents and grandparents of support..

31 See Hoghughi, M. (1992) In assessing child and adolescent disorders, Dr Hoghughi outlines important areas of the child's life where difficulties or mal-adaptations can occur. Although the development of the child profile was designed as a diagnostic method in order to plan treatment interventions, we consulted appropriate sections widely during the development of the questionnaire. See also Brimblecombe, F.S.W. et al (1987) a study on disability where key areas of a young persons life were assessed to indicated need or areas of good functoining.

32 Rosenberg, M. (1979) Conceiving the Self. Basic Books, USA.

33 These findings are consistent with the studies of Clark, D. et al (1989) who found that systems in schools for acknowledging and dealing with family problems were usually pragmatic rather than planned.

34 See also Rutter, M. (1989) Re: Protective Factors and Vulnerability.

35 This agrees with data from the Kiernan, K. & Wicks, M. report (1990) but appears to contradict the much larger study of Bradshow, J. (1991) (e.g. a smaller sample maybe an important factor). See also Amato, K. Keith, B. Meta Analysis (1981) and studies by Burghes, L. (1993) and Jacobs, N. & Furstenberg, F. (1986) which looks at the financial status of lone parents and re-married family groups after divorce; two partnered families whether always married or re-married were found to be similar financially and lone-parenthood was much more likely to be associated with poverty. The Jacobs, N. and Furstenberg, F. study also found that factors such as parental conflict/loss of parental relationship and frequent changes of school were also associated with poorer outcomes after divorce.

36 See Capaldi, D. et al (1991) and Peterson, J. & Zill, N. (1986).

37 Also found by Hunter, J. & Schuman, N. (1980).

38 Jenkins, J. & Smith, M. (1990) Factors protecting children in disharmonious homes: Maternal Reports. American Academy of Child and Adolescent Psychiatry: 29.(1);60-69.

39 Rutter, M. (1989) Re: Protective Factors And Vulnerability.

40 Richards, MN. (1982) and Ferri, E. (1976) and Cherlin, A. (1991).

41 This issues has been discussed by Richards, M. (1982). See also previous research section for re-outcomes for boys versus girls and Hodges, W.F. (1986).

42 Camera, K.A. & Resnick, G. (1988) This study looks at conflict pre-divorce, conflicts escalating at the time of separation, and continuing into the post divorce period.

43 Wadsworth, M. et al (1986) and Wallerstein, J. & Kelly, J. (1980) also Fergusson, D., Dimond, M. & Horwood, L. (1986). In the Exeter study, as in some other studies high conflict divorces were associated with more problems for the child (see also New York Longitudinal study 1983) and there is some evidence to suggest from the present study, that the continuing conflict may interfere with the child's relationship with both parents.

44 Wallerstein, J. et al (1989) "Second Chances" and Mitchell, A. (1985) and Walzack, Y. & Burns, S. (1984).

45 Bradshaw, J. (1991) and Fergusson, D. et al (1986) and Shaw & emery, R. (1987) these last two studies found that inter-parental conflict was associated with poor outcomes regardless of family type. Chase-Landsdale, L. et al 1990) and Richards, M. (1987) also support the view of parental conflict as a major negative influence although Richards has always stressed the importance of both biological parents to the child and the need for continued contact.

46 Wadsworth, M.E. & MacLean, M. (1986) Parents' Divorce and children's Life Chances.

47 Wallerstein, J. et al (1989).

48 McLoughlin, D. & Whitfield, R. (1984) Adolescents and their experience of parental divorce: Journal of Adolescence 7:155-170.

49 Mitchell, M. (1985) & Wallerstein, J. & Kelly, J. (1980).

50 See Hetherington, E.M. et al 91986) also Mitchell, M. (1985) and walzack, Y. & burns, S. (1984).

51 Wallerstein, J. & Blakeslee, S. (1989) Second Chances. Men, Women & Children – a Decade after Divorce.

52 Wadsworth, M. (1991). See also Kurdek, L.A. & Berg, B. (1983) and Luepintz, D.A. (1982) which found that children's outcomes were less likely to improve post divorce if conflict between the parents continued.

The Exeter Family Study

Divorce

"When I was younger and left home, I thought paradise existed out there."

Lone mother

"Since my husband left, I have learnt that you are almost always better off with a husband, even with problems, especially if you get ill you need somebody else to fall back on."

Lone mother

An integral part of the study was an examination of the way that divorce and separation had come about for the re-ordered families and how arrangements – especially those for contact between children and their parents –were working out in practice. As in the study of outcomes in Chapter 4, it was considered important to obtain the children's own views of what had happened.

Grounds for divorce

Three out of four families has sought their divorce on grounds that were based one or other partner's alleged "fault" – either adultery or unreasonable behaviour. The separating parents had all seen solicitors, but whereas 87 per cent of resident parents (mostly wives) had been legally aided, the same was true of only half the non-resident parents (mostly husbands). Independent mediation (concerned with children's issues only) has been available in Exeter since 1986, but only four of the 76 families had made any use of the service.

Mothers were more likely to have sought the end of the marriage and to have filed for divorce and fathers were more likely to have left the family home. Most custody orders[1] had been made in favour of the mother, but there were 19 joint custody orders. Mothers had also mostly been granted care and control (pre-Children Act 1989).

A majority (48) of court orders governing contact between children and their non-resident parent were "undefined", pointing to a degree of co-operation between the parents. However, 23 were "defined", indicating that those parents had found it difficult to agree flexible and child-centred arrangements between themselves. This finding may be misleading because, according to research carried out by Pearson (1993), defined access arrangements sometimes work better for the child because parents have less to fight about.[2]

Three-quarters of families claimed to have "sorted out" their finances, although a significant minority (13) had continuing problems, including seven resident parents who said they had debts from the first marriage. Four parents said that there were no problems simply because there was: *"nothing to sort – no house, no money, just the kids."*

One in five resident parents received regular maintenance payments. Children were generally aware of the link between the receipt of maintenance by their mothers and visits to their fathers. A few (5) described being sent specifically to collect money from their non-resident parent or to ask for money for clothes, holidays or to pay bills. It was also found that a small minority of non-resident parents (7) were found to be operating informal agreements with their former spouses. Parents saw this as a way of providing extra money, which would have otherwise not reached the child as it would have been taken into account as maintenance if the parents were on benefit.

Table 5.1 **The End of the Relationship**

N = 76	Mother	Father	Both	Never married	No order
Who filed for divorce	57	14	0	5	0
Who left the house	20	56	0	0	0
Who ended the relationship	51	17	8	0	0
Custody orders made	48	1	19	0	8
Care and control	66	4	0	0	6

Reactions to divorce

Responses to divorce varied according to whether the parent interviewed had chosen to leave the marriage. There was no discrepancy in the versions from either party of the reasons for the end of their marriage, but they often felt very differently about the outcomes, including residence, contact with children and financial matters. Some resident parents reported particularly strong feelings of regret, waste, devastation and anger: *"I could have killed him"*, *"Life will never be the same again"*. A majority of resident and non-resident parents expressed an initial feeling of loneliness at the end of the marriage.[3] The remainder expressed feelings of isolation that they had not expected.

In some circumstances where the wife had asked the husband to leave, fathers felt bewildered by the rejection. This was true even where they felt their own behaviour was to blame. They still believed that their wives should not have ended their relationship and would have liked to have tried again: *"I thought we were a team and discussed things, but it turned out we weren't."*

There was a general feeling expressed by non-resident parents that their difficulties were compounded by a widely held view that they were the ones who had "chosen" to break away and must, therefore, have fewer problems. In different ways resident and non-resident parents had found the process of surrendering their partner relationship while maintaining their parenting relationship particularly painful: *"I didn't expect to have all the responsibility for the children."* Or conversely: *"Their mother wouldn't let them have a relationship with me, she fought me for the children."* Non-resident fathers also reported difficulties associated with starting life again as a single person: *"It was like being adolescent and free, but not really wanting it."*

Resident parents were, on the whole, more negative about the future than non-resident parents. Some women, nevertheless, described divorce as a positive experience. They considered themselves to be more independent, accusing their husbands of not having allowed them a life of their own. A number of women said they had felt a strong sense of freedom when their marriage was over: *"I was thrilled – it was just what I wanted."* But only three of the non-resident parents interviewed – including two mothers – said they actively preferred life as a "part-time parent". Almost three out of four said they regretted the end of their marriage or cohabitation and felt it was "a waste".

Parents nevertheless recognised that although life might be better for them, their children did not always hold the same view: *"They've got second best."* Seventy per cent of the non-resident parents interviewed described their children as being very upset by their departure from the home, and over half said that they were aware that their children had not wanted the marriage to end. Only four non-resident parents felt that things were better for their children than they had been.

A sizeable minority said that separation from their children was worse than they had expected: *"You miss out on them growing up – you've lost that time and you can't get it back."* Five said that they would have liked to have had their children living them and three expressed concerns about the child's welfare with the resident parent.

Many non-resident parents would have liked to have had a more active role in their children's schooling; most did not feel that the school encouraged their contact. Even so, there were several (8), who expressed a view that they felt that they had no right to be involved with their children's lives beyond a certain level: *"I ask him questions and the answers are slow in coming". "I don't pry – it's not my business any more."*

Continuing conflict

In just under half (34) of the re-ordered families major rows (involving one parent leaving the house, throwing things or violence) were recalled during their first marriage (Table 5.2). Of those recalling serious rows only 7 had no major conflict after separation. Of those 41 who had less

Table 5.2 **Conflict during first marriage**

Conflict since separation	No rows	Normal rows	Major rows	Totals
No major conflict	0	20	7	27
Early conflict	0	6	9	15
Continuing conflict	1	15	18	34
Totals	**1**	**41**	**34**	**76**

The Exeter Family Study

serious rows ("normal" in Table 5.2 including shouting, prolonged silences, etc.) during their relationship, 21 have had major conflict since their separation, of which 15 continue in conflict. From the child's perspective conflict associated with parental separation, was therefore reduced in 7 families, but increased or continued in 49 though subsequently reduced over time in 15 of these. In 17 families continuing conflict had resulted in loss of regular contact for the child.

It was evident that in a number of cases the notion of "winners and losers" in divorce was actively hindering adaptation to changed circumstances – *"I got the bills, she got the house"* – for adults and for children.[4] Conflict had in many instances (47) continued after the divorce but had improved over time for some families (35 families still had problems at the time of interview, including 17 where contact had ceased). Only four out of ten divorced or separated parents in the study found it possible to talk to each other at all easily about arrangements for their children without feelings of anger, resentment, frustration or, in some cases, fear.[5] Another two out of ten said that there were difficulties in communication and the remainder did not speak to their ex-spouses at all. Of those parents who *were* able to talk to their former partners, nearly half said that the levels of communication had improved over time.

Anecdotal information highlighted the fact that in most cases arrangements for the children might have been better if communication had been more clearly established. As many as 14 children had felt obliged to take the initiative in making visiting arrangements because their parents could not reach agreement themselves. Others had found themselves acting as "go-betweens": *"Everything is all right as long as I don't let Mum and Dad speak to each other."* It was, perhaps, not surprising that children whose parents continued to have a poor relationship after separation and divorce tended to have lower self-esteem than children whose parents had made good arrangements (Figure 5.1).[6]

Preparing the children

From talking to children it was clear that most (66) had been well aware of conflict in their parents' relationship before they actually separated.[7] Only one in nine who were old enough to remember said they had not realised how bad the situation prior to divorce had become. Most parents agreed that their children had been aware of the deterioration, although as many as one in six

Figure 5.1 **Lowered self-esteem as measured in children where contact arrangements were difficult after divorce.**

In this figure the percent of children with lowered self-esteem is shown for re-ordered families according to the presence (Y, back row) or absence (N, front row) of three areas of parental difficulty.

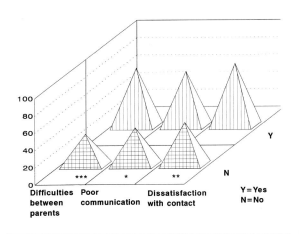

denied that this was the case.

Even so, it emerged that only five (6 per cent) of the 76 children in re-ordered families had received a joint explanation about the departure of one parent from the family home before it actually happened. Another six children had received separate explanations from both their parents and seven had been told about the break-up by both parents together – but only after the non-resident parent had moved out.

Nevertheless, in over seven out of ten families it had been left to the mother (the usual resident parent) to tell children that their father had left. Moreover, in eight of the families under study, it appeared that children had received no explanation whatever, and that another 16 had been told little more than the fact of their father's departure. Parents in these latter cases had either believed that their child was too young to understand or that further explanation was unnecessary.[8]

Children were generally aware of their parents' feelings following divorce: *"When Dad left, Mum didn't know what she was going to do."* Many, however, found it difficult to say which parent had been most upset by the divorce. Slightly more who expressed a view one way or the other believed it was their father. Nine thought that both parents were equally hurt and 15 believed that neither parent was upset.[9]

Contact arrangements

"Older children will decide which parent needs them most"

The parents of the study children in re-ordered families usually acknowledged that their child had gone through a time of crisis immediately after separation.[10] Nevertheless, two-thirds of both resident and non-resident parents believed that their child was now coping well with the altered family situation. The remaining third identified continuing problems that made it difficult for their children to adapt – although they were often unsure of what could be done to make things better for them.

Seven out of ten children in re-ordered families (54) had at least some contact with their non-resident parent. Parents mostly recognised that their children had mixed feelings about whatever arrangements existed for them to visit. They observed how children often (43) began by not wanting to leave home, but were then reluctant to return when it was time for the visit to end.[10] *"She will say one time that she never wants to see her dad again and another time that she wants to see him, so she's ambivalent, but it obviously plays on her mind."* Not unexpectedly, it was common for both parents to maintain that they were the one that their child *really* wanted to be with. Six out of ten non-resident parents said that they found these "transfer times" stressful.

Parents had also, for the most part, noticed that their children found it difficult to talk to them about time spent with the other parent. Only one in five (5) said that their children could talk freely about life at home with their former partner. Even this, however, presented a more optimistic picture than the account given by children themselves (see below). Non-resident parents were more likely to suggest their child had a problem talking freely than resident parents.[11]

Most resident parents and almost half the non-resident parents interviewed (11) said they missed their children during the times when they were not with them; the remainder said they had got used to it or accepted it. Only a minority (three non-resident parents) claimed to prefer spending less time with their children: *"I don't want any more contact than I have got. I never wanted to be a parent, I like not being a full-time parent."*[12]

Resident parents

There were a number who believed that contact arrangements had improved over time. A third (32 per cent) said they were dissatisfied now compared with over half (55 per cent) who said they had been dissatisfied at the time of divorce. Even so, only 14 (18 per cent) of resident parents said their children had regular contact with their former spouse with which there were no problems. Another 27 (36 per cent) reported a range of reasons for considering the contact unreliable: they complained that non-resident parents did not always turn up, that the visits were not frequent enough for the child, or that contact was so brief that they could not make sensible alternative use of the time themselves.

In cases where contact had broken down completely (10), some resident parents were happy that their ex-partner had stayed away. Others (7), however, would have liked more contact and shared responsibility.

Non-resident parents

Those interviewed were more likely to express dissatisfaction with current contact arrangements (17 out of 26). Complaints included wanting more time and also wanting opportunities to see children individually (where there was more than one) as well as together. Nine parents (one in three) reported that lack of proper accommodation was a factor making it difficult to make good quality contact arrangements. More said this had been a problem when the marriage first broke up.

However, more than half also said there were no problems putting the current arrangements into practice. One in four said that arrangements were working out better than they had been at the time of the initial breakdown.

Children's views

"I felt left down when I was young, Dad forgot us."

Of the 54 children (71 per cent) in re-ordered families who had any sort of contact with their non-resident parent, very few felt positive about the arrangements. Most described their own "comings and goings" between parents as either negative or, at best, "all right". Only four claimed to find the transfer between one parent and another at all easy and most described it as stressful.

Contact arrangements had, in most cases, been agreed between the parents without consulting the child. The majority of children (55) not only felt that they should have been involved, especially the older age group, but also considered that this could have reduced tension and hostility between their parents. As it stood, they had no control over the plans and had to "fit in" with whatever had been decided for them. About half the group said that they would have liked to see their non-resident parent more often.

Just under half were broadly satisfied with the way that the contact arrangements were working out. These included 14 children who had made their own arrangements because communications between their parents had broken down (see Chapter 4). The remainder either accepted the constraints on their contact or were actively unhappy about it.

Fewer than half the children (34) said that they saw their non-resident parent regularly, ("at least once a month"), and of those only 10 were in contact more than once a week. Seven children regularly "popped in" or lived near enough "to cycle over" or call in on their way home from school without a formal arrangement. Five children regularly spent overnight visits with their non-resident parent during the school week. Just six reckoned to spend more than half the weekends in the year with their non-resident parent.

A small group of children had regularly seen their non-resident parent for a short time after divorce but found that arrangements gradually became less reliable. Feelings about this were mixed. One child told the interviewers: *"I used to want a new Dad, but not now."* But another said: *"He came to visit us and shouted at us, so I don't want to see him again."*

Almost eight out of ten of those children (54) who saw their non-resident parent regularly, if not always frequently said that they did not find it easy to talk to one parent about the other, and most of the remainder (14) said they never mentioned the other parent at all: *"I've learnt to keep quiet when I come home."*

In one in four re-ordered families (20) neither the child nor the resident parent knew where the other parent was living. This included 17 who had no contact with the non-resident parent whatsoever (two children met their father twice a year in town and one child had only seen him by knocking on the door after 3 years of no contact to ask why he had not been in touch). Lack of contact was not always related to distance – some non-resident parents lived locally but still did not keep in touch.

Parents' new partners

Most of the 27 non-resident parents interviewed had begun a new relationship (not all live in) since parting with the resident parent. Their children tended to feel that they received not enough information about new partners: *"Dad got married and didn't tell us – he shouldn't have done that."* Feelings expressed about both fathers' and mothers' new partners often revealed confusion and ambivalence. Only three children whose parents had formed new relationships were really positive about them.

Children who had been through multiple family disruption, meanwhile, not only described problems about visiting their biological fathers, but had also, in a significant minority of cases (10), lost contact with a step-parent figure and any half or step-brothers and sisters.[13]

Telephone and postal contact

"Contact" was defined in the interviews as face to face visits with the non-resident parent. Other forms of contact were explored anecdotally. However, in the 17 cases where children reported no contact visits with the non-resident parent, it transpired that there was also no contact by telephone or letter. Where contact was described as rare, it appeared that children sometimes received letters and cards at Christmas and a telephone call "out of the blue" to arrange a visit: *"We get a phone call every 2 years or so, when he happens to be in the country, but mostly we don't know where he is."*

Most non-resident parents who were spending time with their children on a regular basis also telephoned them (usually about arrangements), and sent cards and letters when away on business trips or holidays. This kind of contact had sometimes proved difficult if communications between the parents remained poor. Although welcomed by the child, telephone contact, letters, cards and presents could be seen as threatening and undermining by the resident parent: *"I know it's Mum on the phone, because his voice goes all cold and he holds the phone away from him."* In one particular case, renewed contact by post after many years was proving difficult for both resident parent and child. As the mother explained: *"I know she's building up her hopes – she keeps the letters in her bedroom."*

Children reported they would also sometimes telephone their non-resident parent or send cards to them. They telephoned about making arrangements or *"when things happened, like* when I pass an exam or when I need something." Children felt an obvious need to share their successes and failures with their non-resident parent, where possible, but in some cases, they were also conscious of their parent's lack of interest. Children who did it usually said they found it reassuring to keep in touch in this way. There was, nevertheless, a feeling was that resident parents did not encourage it, although it had not been openly discussed .

Some grandparents who no longer saw their grandchildren because of separation, also telephoned and wrote to them. They also sent cards and presents for Christmas and birthdays. Although most resident parents welcomed this, a small proportion were resentful and felt it represented minimum interest rather than a genuine desire to keep in touch.[14]

Domestic violence

"I used to lock the boys in the bedroom before he came home, so that they wouldn't see."

Previous marital violence was reported by one in four re-ordered families (20). Two levels of violence were reported. In some cases, there had been a long history of domestic assaults (as long as children could remember, in some cases). Alternatively, parents and children described short episodes of violence that precipitated or followed a decision to bring the marriage to an end.[15]

Mothers who had experienced violence spoke of living in fear while the marriage lasted. Children also reported being terrified by that they could hear taking place: "I used to hide myself away in the smallest part of my bedroom." Women victims who had separated from violent men regarded the break as the chance to begin a new life. In four instances, however, mothers had been subjected to violence after separation during the course of contact visits.

Three mothers had taken their children to the women's refuge (two of whom felt that the refuge had not afforded them sufficient protection against their violent partners). Two others – rare examples of non-resident mothers in the study – said they had left the family home without their children because of marital violence. As other studies have found[16] there appeared to be no cohesive approach to helping the victim of marital violence, the instigator or the child.

After violent relationships had ended, children in the study were especially unlikely to have been told the whereabouts of their absent parent.

Yet few had been given any explanation as to why contact was difficult. Parents who had experienced domestic violence said they would have welcomed clearer guidelines and processes to deal with the end of violent marriages and subsequent arrangements for the children.

It was also apparent that disputes over contact and property between parents at the time of divorce had thrown-up something of a smoke screen, making it less likely that the issues of physical violence and child abuse would be taken into account.

Allegations were sometimes made during the divorce process about violence and child abuse that were not proven. Resident parents, themselves afraid of the violent partner, said in this study that there was little protection in law to assist the organisation of contact after violence. Other issues became more important once parents were separated. One in 16 children (7) were found to be still in contact with an allegedly violent parent, and three of the study children continued to live with one. It seemed possible, therefore, that residence and contact arrangements had been reached which in a few cases involved risks to children's safety.[17] "I don't mind them visiting him now he has got a girlfriend and as long as the children go together."

Conversely, it was possible that non-resident parents who ought to have been seeing their children might have be prevented from doing so by unproved allegations of abuse.

1   Pre the Children Act (1989).

2   See Pearson, J. (1993), which found that some parents preferred and responded better to "defined" contact orders. This arrangement caused less difficulty between parents than making their own arrangements, there was less ground for disagreement.

3   Weiss, R. (1975). This study showed that partners harbour ambivalent feelings towards their spouses after the decision to part has been made, even though they chose to end the relationship. See also Wallerstein, J. & Kelly, J. (1980).

4   Wallerstein, J. & Blakeslee, S. (1989) Some parents in this qualitative follow-up of 15 families had adapted well, not only those who had chosen to leave the marriage. Others had remained saddened and over burdened by their new role, either as resident parent or as a lonely non-resident parent (usually father).

5   See Hetherington, E.M. et al. (1986) and the Amato, P. & Bruce, K. (1991) meta Analysis for discussion about the effects and duration and nature of conflict during and post-divorce. See also Hodges. W.F. (1986) for discussion of early studies which show that children may fuel conflict to enforce contact between parents and effect a reconciliation.

6   See discussion in Emery, R. (1988) where studies by Raschke, J.H. & Raschke, V.J. (1979) found no difference between intact and re-ordered families in measures of self-concept. Slater, E. & Haber, J. (1984) also found this, though both studies report correlation between high levels of parental conflict and low self-esteem regardless of family status.

7   See Mitchell, A. (1985) whose qualitative study also found that children were aware of parental rows but had not expected their parents to separate.

8 Both Hetherington, E.M. et al. (1981) and Mitchell, A. (1985) found that children were badly prepared for parental separation.

9 See Mitchell, A. (1985) and Wallerstein, J. & Blakeslee, S. (1989) for childrens' qualitative accounts of parental distress.

10 See also Hetherington, E.M. et al. (1986) and Wallerstein, J. & Blakeslee, S. (1989) for qualitative accounts of childrens' accounts of their own acute distress at the time of their parents' separation.

10 Johnson, J.R., Campbell, L.E.G. & Mayes, S.S. (1985). See also Warshak, R. & Santrock, J. (1983) The impact of divorce in father custody and mother custody homes. The Child's Perspective in L.A. Kurdek and B. Berg (1983) and Hirst, S.R. & Smiley, G.W. (1984).

11 See Hodges, W.F. (1986) re: studies about the child's ability to cope with conflict at different ages and the importance of quality of contact. Children in the Exeter study complained of boring, inconsistent, and irregular contact.

12 See Pasley, K. & Ihinger-Tallman, M. (1987) re: the nature of part-time parenting and parents' response to it. This present study shows that the majority of non-resident parents were not well prepared for part-time parenting.

13 There were children in the Exeter study who lost contact with several sets of grandparents and particularly older step-brothers or sisters, who may not have lived with the child in the parental home. Children whose non-resident fathers had repartnered and who had no contact with the study child also had step- and half-brothers and sisters whom they did not know.

14 Adoption law and practices in social work are also being influenced since the Children Act (1989), which places the emphasis on enduring parental responsibility and the necessity and desirability of fostering links with natural parents whenever possible. There is also a growing acceptance that children can maintain good but different relationships with both natural, adoptive and/or surrogate parents according to the age and understanding of the child.

15 See Hestor, M. & Radford, L. (1992).

16 See Kelly, J. (1981) and Yellot A. (1990). There are programmes under way in some parts of the country to support the rehabilitation of families after violent relationships have ended, mainly through the Probation Service but are better developed in the USA, though not widespread. Parents who had experienced violent marriages felt unprotected in this present study.

17 See Erikson, S. & McKnight, M. (1990) re: mediating families where there has been domestic violence.

Services

"I thought I was the only one going through divorce and I felt a failure. I had no family and I would have liked a friend or someone at a doctor's surgery or a solicitor's office or some literature. The two main ports of call are the GP and the solicitor and information should be available there – there was none for me."

Both parents and children were asked about any support they had received from within their family circle, from informal networks or through outside agencies, if either the family or the child had experienced difficulties. Parents who had been separated and divorced said they had known little about the divorce process and how best to address the task of arranging their children's future. Most had been confused about their own rights and responsibilities and had been afraid of "the unknown", including doubts about their own ability to cope alone.[1]

Parents were also conscious of a reduced capacity to take sensible decisions during the initial stages of breakdown, when they found themselves under particular stress. They tended to have clear views about ways that the available services could be made more helpful. Children, by contrast, were more confused. Children were aware of their parents' difficulties at the time of separation and divorce and approximately half said that they would have valued talking to someone about this. Again approximately half said that they talked to their parents at home, but were aware that there were some things best not discussed at home: *"I have learnt to keep quiet when I come home"*. Some children talked to friends at school, some to teachers.

Informal support

"Once you start divorce proceedings you should know where to go for help, not only financial, but keeping your head together, how to deal with loneliness."

As might be expected, parents in intact families tended to support their partners – nearly seven out of ten said that they relied on the other parent most for support; the remainder said they

Table 6.1 **Family Support**

	Intact	Single	Step	Re-disrupted
		(n = 31)	(n = 26)	(n = 19)
New partner /original	52	1 ("not live in")	15	7
Family/friends	21	28	11	12
No-one	3	2	0	0

depended on extended family (mostly grandparents) and friends.

Parents who had experienced separation and divorce were more likely to rely on their extended families for support. This was true not only of the vast majority of lone parents, but also of a substantial minority of those who were living with new partners (Table 6.1). But even looking back to the time when they and their child's other parent were together, they recalled a lower level of dependence on their partner than that described by families that were still intact. Some also reported how support from grandparents and others had been abruptly withdrawn from them at the time of separation as relatives "took sides".[2]

When asked what kind of help had been most useful, half the re-ordered families said "emotional support". The same was true of only one in five intact families. Intact families viewed "practical help" as more important (Figure 6.1).

Figure 6.1 **Parents' view of the kinds of help that were most useful**

In this figure the study group is divided into rows, re-ordered (back row) and intact (front row) families showing the levels and kinds of help useful to families.

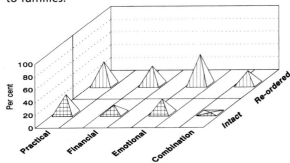

Some parents described the divorce process as being caught in a chain of events over which they felt they had no control. This had reduced their decision making power at a time when they were being called upon to make important choices for their future. Changed circumstances in these cases seemed to have "paralysed" parents and lessened their ability to seek help.

Children's sources of support

More children in intact families (49) than re-ordered families (38) said that they had never felt the need to talk to someone else about their problems. Of the children who said that they had particular problems, 30 per cent had talked to "someone, not a parent", more were found in re-ordered than intact families.

Overall, children were more likely to describe themselves as supportive to their brothers and sisters than to tell the researchers that they had received any help from siblings themselves. Slightly more children in intact families reported being supportive to their siblings than in re-ordered families. Sisters were rather more likely to have talked to their siblings than brothers. A sizeable minority (15) of children in re-disrupted and step-families said that they were supportive to half- or step-brothers and sisters. Other research has shown that sibling support grows stronger during periods of inadequate parenting.[3]

One in four children in the study said they discussed their problems with friends at school and just under a third said that they talked to teachers and other staff: *"It helped to talk to someone – it used to go round in my head."*

Children in re-ordered families were more likely to have done both. According to their teachers they were more likely to have been openly distressed in school. More children said they had talked to their teachers than parents were aware of. But this did not amount to formal help being available to children from re-ordered families.[4]

Formal support services

Parents in the study families had sought help from a range of different services. Their broadly positive or negative experiences of seeking and receiving support are recorded in Table 6.2.

Intact families

Intact families had made far fewer approaches for formal advice and support than re-ordered families; 35 requests for help made by 15 different intact families compared with 146 requests made by 45 re-ordered families. All of the re-ordered families had used legal services at some time and the vast majority had felt positive about the help received from other services. Intact families had approached lawyers for, among other things, conveyancing services and about compensation claims. Most reported positive experiences.

Despite the fact that 22 intact families reported serious marital problems (out of 35 reporting conflict), only two had approached Relate for marriage guidance, one finding it more helpful than the other. Those intact families who had sought help from the Citizen's Advice Bureau or the Department of Social Security tended to be more positive about the experience than the much higher number of re-ordered families who had done the same.

Table 6.2 **Families' view of help received from services**

	Intact			Re-ordered (Resident parents)		
	Not used	Help received		Not used	Help received	
		Positive	Negative		Positive	Negative
Lawyers	53	19	4	0	63	13
Social Services	72	4	0	50	19	7
Probation	75	1	0	60	9	7
Mediation*	0	0	0	72	4	0
Relate	74	1	1	62	11	3
CAB	60	14	2	49	23	4
DSS	63	8	5	17	34	25

Re-ordered families

Re-ordered families said that their need for easily accessible support services had varied at different stages (see Case Histories in Chapter 4).

- *The acute stage* – advice, information and support (e.g. GPs, Citizen's Advice, Relate).

- *The intermediate stage* – services to resolve the situation (e.g. lawyers, mediation).

- *Long-term as a result of change* – long-term support (e.g. Gingerbread; the Step-family Association) or family therapy or psychiatric support.

Solicitors, family doctors and school staff were the professionals that parents in re-ordered families were most likely to have approached about family change.

Community health services

Half of all parents said that their GP was the "most supportive professional" to the family. However, twice as many re-ordered families had sought support from family doctors about family problems at the time of interview than intact families. Over half the parents in re-ordered families said that these consultations were due to family change. Although they generally found their family doctors supportive, a few re-ordered families complained that they did not get referred on for help when they asked for it.

A small number of parents had approached their family health visitor. Most said they found this helpful but one or two reported coming under inappropriate pressure: *"She said I should get divorced, it would be best for me."* Two families said that a family therapist had been helpful, but in five other instances where family therapy had been tried, the children had refused to go for individual sessions.

Solicitors

Marriage is a contract in law and its dissolution, in most cases, needs professional legal advice. Most parents in re-ordered families (63) said their lawyers had been helpful: *"He couldn't have been nicer, he came round and took me to court by car."* But for a minority (13) they were judged to have made a bad situation worse. Some families said the complicated language and protocol used by lawyers had contributed to their confusion.

Most separated parents, nevertheless, recognised that their solicitors had tried to keep the family needs and the needs of the child at the centre of negotiation while safeguarding their client's interest. A few, however, had been distinguished by their adversarial tenacity: *"We would meet and agree things, she would go to her solicitor and he would say – you must be mad."* Non-resident parents were generally more prone to complain about lack of support from their lawyers than resident parents. Their feelings were often compounded by having had to find alternative accommodation and pay maintenance.

In the majority of divorce cases the parents had received Legal Aid, but this encompassed just 51 per cent of non-resident parents compared with 87 per cent of resident parents. This was a further source of resentment for men whose former wives had been legally aided, when they had not. It was also found that, in a number of cases, parents had been unaware of their liability to repay legal fees once they had realised capital assets, including the sale of the family home: *"The legal system milks you and gets what it can from you."*

Social Services

Two thirds of those who had approached social services (30) had found them helpful, but several families expressed fear of involving social workers in case their children were taken into care: *"They were nice to the children, but not to me. I was afraid."* Other mothers said they were afraid to admit they could no longer cope. Contact between intact families and social services had been minimal and was rated positively by the four families concerned.

Social Security

Thirteen intact families compared with 59 re-ordered families had been in current or recent contact with the DSS. Although larger numbers of re-ordered families were receiving benefits, about one in four recipients in both groups reported a "bad experience" (stronger words were sometimes used, such as "insulting", "demeaning" and "pitiful"). Even so, more families found the DSS helpful than unhelpful.

A higher proportion of re-ordered families than currently intact families had received benefits *before* the separation. Nevertheless, for a significant number of families, divorce or separation marked the first time that they had needed to ask the State for financial support. There were complaints that benefits took a long time to arrive, that families were often without money in between payments and that there had been no attempt to make them aware of their entitlement to extra benefits. Mothers with young children had also found appointments at the local office stressful because the waiting time was usually long. In only one instance had a home visit had been made to a re-ordered family.

Probation family welfare services

Sixteen re-ordered families had been in contact with the probation service or a court welfare officer during divorce proceedings, among whom seven reported a negative experience. In-court mediation services are used by approximately 300 to 400 families a year in the Exeter area (1,000 decrees nisi are granted per year by the Exeter courts) but parents in the study were not very clear about the service. Only two said they had "attended a meeting" with a probation service mediator, while a larger proportion of families had been made the subject of a welfare report requested by the court.

It was also evident that the parents who found the court welfare officer's work most helpful were those who had obtained an outcome of which they approved. Non-resident fathers in particular did not feel greatly supported and felt that their cause was lost before they began: *"We had a joint meeting with the probation officer at the family home and my youngest son hurt himself and came running to his mother. That's the moment I lost the custody case and my wife agreed with me, afterwards."*

There was a feeling that decisions were made on insufficient evidence of parental suitability, and that the status quo situation detracted from the non-resident parent's chances of being heard.[5]

Mediation

Independent services to help couples reach mutual agreement about the arrangements for their children were available locally, but only four families had made use of them. The role of mediation appeared to be poorly understood by parents and professionals alike. Although 17 re-ordered families had heard of mediation (or conciliation), most had not seen the service as an alternative way of sorting our their own problems. The majority of parents, especially non-resident parents, were surprised to learn that such a service existed. The handful of families who had attended independent mediation found it helpful, although they did not appear to have taken on board the need, underlined by the mediators, that they

should remain in contact with their ex-partner. Approximately 100 families per year apply to the Exeter independent services for help.[6]

Relate

Fourteen re-ordered families and two intact families had visited Relate. Most had found the service helpful (although four did not). Eleven of the 76 re-ordered families had used the marriage guidance service prior to separation.[7]

Citizen's Advice Bureaux

A third of re-ordered families reported visiting a Citizen's Advice Bureau (four having a negative experience) compared with one in five intact families (two of whom failed to find the service helpful). Families had approached the Citizen's Advice Bureaux for information about using other services and about debts.

Other services

A small number of parents reported positive contact with other services, including the Samaritans (two fathers who had felt suicidal), and a local disability support unit (one family). Individual families also mentioned speech therapy, Victim Support and the Women's Voluntary Service.

Services parents would have liked

Better communication

Some parents wanted help in achieving better, more reliable contact, with the non-resident parent. Children said that parents should talk to each other and parents themselves identified the need for "family relationships to be better". But although they recognised the relevance of better communication, parents did not identify mediation services as being a possible source of help.

Explanations about divorce

Parents often wanted advice on how best to explain divorce and separation to their children, other relatives and to school teachers. Explaining about the family changes was painful to them and some parents still felt that family breakdown carried a social stigma.

Housing improvements

A desire for more space, better heating, less damp, less mould, and suitable play areas were reported most often by re-ordered families. Most families at the time of separation and divorce had been obliged to move into less satisfactory housing, in many cases provided through special local authority agreements with housing associations. In some cases, the local authority was accused of being slow to respond to requests for repairs.

Debt counselling

Debts relating to low income and unemployment were a problem for both intact (16) and re-ordered families (41). Serious debts were reported by two intact families, ten re-ordered resident parents and approximately half of non-resident parents.

DSS home visits

Parents complained that it was expensive and time-consuming to take public transport into the centre of town with children (34 per cent had no car) to gain information about benefits. In one instance the DSS had made a home visit, but the majority of parents had to find their own way to the offices.

Domestic violence

Some families who had experienced separation and divorce which involved violence said they needed a safer refuge than those available. Those who worked with the victims of domestic violence agreed that more use could be made of legal restraining injunctions, and that there was a need to improve the available services which, at present, parents felt did not afford them adequate protection. The resources to do this were said to be unavailable.

1   Hetherington, E.M. et al. (1986) and Wallerstein, J. & Kelly, J. (1980). See previous research section re parenting in the immediate post-divorce stage, while parents adapt to a new status.

2   See Hodges, W.F. (1986) The non-resident parent grandparents are typically in less contact with their grandchildren; if the non-resident parent loses touch with his children, the resident parent may choose to cease contact with the non-resident grandparents, because it is too painful for both parent and child.

3   See Bank, S. & Kahan, D. (1982), which looks at the increasing need for siblings to support each other as parental support for children decreases because of their pre-occupation with their own problems in the immediate post-divorce period.

4   Wallerstein, J. & Kelly, J. (1980) also discuss the importance of school support and the parents lack of awareness of the child's ad hoc support from their teachers.

5   See Pearson, J. (1993). This paper explores the truth or otherwise of parental behaviours or views of services after divorce and their satisfaction with outcomes. See also Pearson, J. (1991).

6   An evaluation of the service by the Department of Child Health in 1989 found that parental satisfaction with the service was directly linked to their ability to reach agreement with their partner.

7   The Relate Marriage Guidance Council in Exeter provides services for between 700 and 800 couples a year, but at present there are no statistics about the numbers of couples who remain together or who go on to separate following counselling by the service.

Discussion

Social changes affecting families have made it more likely that the needs of parents will not always coincide with those of their children. Growing separation of the roles of "parent" and "partner", women's reduced economic dependence on male partners and the diminished importance of marriage as a key transition into adulthood, are among the relevant contributing factors. Any disparity between the wishes and needs of children and those of their parents is, however, liable to be most acute in circumstances surrounding separation and divorce.[1]

There is a large and rapidly expanding literature on the effects of marital breakdown on children.[2] Studies conducted largely in the USA, but also in the UK and other countries, have used a number of completely different approaches to the problem.[3] Some of the most useful information comes from longitudinal studies such as the National Survey of Children[4] in the USA, the National Survey of Health and Development (the 1946 cohort)[5] and the National Child Development Study (the 1958 cohort)[6] in the UK. A further cohort study in New Zealand has yielded useful data and comparisons.[7] In the UK, Michael Rutter has also conducted population-based studies using school-based cohorts, groups of children in care, young people leaving care and clinical samples.[8]

These studies have found significant adverse outcomes associated with parental divorce. This is true both in the medium term, with effects on children's physical and psychological health, education and behaviour, and in the longer term, where young people's chances of leaving school without qualifications and their risks of teenage pregnancy, out-of-wedlock births and of early (and relatively brief) marital relationships, are greater than those of children whose families remain intact. The differences are sometimes small, but these effects have been measured not only through childhood into adult life, but also as probable secondary cross-generational effects on the children of children whose parents separated.[9]

Large cohort studies can measure even small effects as statistically significant, and their findings may also be very robust as a large number of possible confounding variables can be controlled for in the analysis. On the other hand, sheer size may mean they are limited as to the number and type of questions that can be asked. The questionnaires may either be self-completed or administered by interviewers, who are not always practitioners with relevant expertise. Smaller-scale studies can, therefore, play a useful role in helping to provide more detailed explanation or qualification for effects that have been observed in big longitudinal studies. In the USA, for example, Wallerstein and Kelly have published a series of reports from their clinical studies of families and children of divorcing parents in California.[10] Theirs, and other qualitative studies, such as those carried out by Walzak and Burns (1984) in England, and Mitchell (1984) in Scotland, have provided important insights and hypotheses. Such work, especially that of Wallerstein and Kelly, has been criticised for being insufficiently quantitative but has, nevertheless, been enormously important in shaping the protocols of subsequent quantitative cross-sectional and longitudinal studies, and in contributing to the debate about the psychological responses to, and effects of, parental separation and divorce. More systematically constructed American research includes the longtitudinal studies of Hetherington and colleagues,[11] Block and colleagues[12] and Guidibaldi and colleagues (1986).[13] Other important reports to which we refer are Peterson & Zill (1986),[14] Capaldi and colleagues (1991)[15] and the study done in Australia by McLoughlin & Whitfield (1984), with adolescents.[16]

None of these studies claim, or even suggest, that adverse effects on children are universal or automatic. They recognise:

- That there may be very important positive outcomes – particularly as, for some families, divorce means the end of a period of immense strain, in many cases associated with violence perpetrated by one partner (usually the father).

- That a number of other factors may ameliorate outcomes or even completely protect some children from the adverse effects seen in others.[17] Rutter, in particular, has written extensively about adverse life events and protective factors, their inter-relationships and children's vulnerability and resilience. Rutter's studies (and the work of other researchers) set out to see not *whether* children of divorced parents had measurably poorer outcomes in their lives, but to try to establish which factors were most closely associated with greater difficulties.[18]

The two most obvious associations with divorce are *parental conflict*, which often precedes and accompanies separation, and the sometimes dramatic *changes in socio-economic status* and *well-being* experienced by the parent caring for the child(ren). Of these, parental conflict has proved to have by far the closest association with any difficulties experienced by children. The general conclusion to be drawn from a review of this literature is that high levels of conflict, particularly where violence is involved, are closely associated with poorer outcomes for children.[19] Some studies have shown that measurable behavioural difficulties can be identified in high conflict families before the breakdown of the marriage, and may even largely explain any later effects of family disruption.[20] Indeed, it might be expected from a common-sense view that the quality of parenting is likely to be compromised in an environment of conflict as parents concentrate on problems concerning their own emotional needs. However, as high levels of conflict and divorce tend to occur in the same families, it has proved extremely difficult to separate their effects, and different reviewers of the same literature have come to different conclusions.[21]

The Exeter Study

The research described in this report was a pilot study to discover whether families in the UK, selected at random from a demographically representative population, would be willing to volunteer and to participate in a very time-consuming and potentially stressful interview about their private family lives. The data shows that families were not only able but willing and enthusiastic about participating.

First, potential participants were invited to complete an initial questionnaire sent out, on the researchers' behalf, by head teachers in all the schools in one area of a small English city (Exeter).[22] The response rate to this initial "cold call" questionnaire was very satisfactory, at over 70 per cent, and it included representative numbers of all socio-economic groups and different housing status, comparable to General Household Survey data for the city. Substantial numbers of re-ordered families (30.4 per cent) responded (which may be an over-representation of such families given that, to receive a questionnaire, they had to have a child of under 13 in the household). The refusal rate to the invitation for full participation by interview of the resident parent(s), child and non-resident parents, was extremely low, and refusals because of unwillingness almost nil.

The response of the families to the interviews also proved almost universally positive, with a majority of families not only pleased to have the opportunity to "tell their story", but also expressing views about the importance of the project and their own relative ignorance, in advance of separation, of the problems that they and their children might face. There were numerous requests for information about the results of the study and offers to participate in any further work. Non-resident parents were particularly keen to be involved once the safeguards of confidentiality were explained and feelings of inadequacy had been addressed by the interviewers.

The method of sampling meant that the authors were able to include most types of re-ordered families, including those headed by fathers, those where multiple reorganisations had taken place ("re-disrupted families"), and those from the lower socio-economic groups, all or some of whom have been excluded from other, otherwise excellent, studies.[23] The Exeter study population does not, however, enable results to be generalised – even to the UK as a whole – not least because the city holds disproportionately few families from different ethnic groups.

The study population was restricted to two age groups, 9–10 years and 13–14 years, on the basis that they were easily contacted through school and were at an age when educational difficulties at school present in different ways. At primary school (9–10-year-olds), learning difficulties are often not apparent or are managed within a standard classroom setting, whereas by 13–14 years, significant under-performance in secondary school is more obvious and may result in additional, specialist help. The authors' clinical experience was that behavioural difficulties at school often present at these ages when they are associated with mild or specific learning difficulties, which may be exacerbated by other events in children's lives.

The study, so far as can be ascertained, represents the first time that so precise a matching of children from re-ordered and intact families has been attempted. Individual children were successfully matched in pairs using six criteria including age, sex, mother's education, position in family, type of school and social class group. The first aim of the matching was to reduce the confounding effects of variables unrelated to family re-organisation that might be sampled unevenly without this precaution. The second aim was to achieve a population of families in the intact family group that matched the family characteristics of the re-ordered family before separation and divorce occurred. In this respect, the inclusion of "social class group of head of household" in the criteria was an attempt to ensure that the data could not be criticised for an "over-correction". However, it introduces a bias that would be expected to result in our findings being an under-estimate of any financial or socio-economic effects in the data.

This report could not examine a number of factors which, it is recognised, may have important effects in understanding the links between the variables studied and the outcomes. The numbers in this study are small and further analysis would be needed to see if it is possible to elucidate differences that have been reported in previous research relating to the age and sex of the child, their position in the family, and the time since divorce. However, the matching process means that the age, sex and position in the family do not influence the outcomes between matched pairs of children and their families.

Time since divorce

Only five out of 76 children in the study group of re-ordered families were in the first year of parental separation, four of them showing signs of acute distress. Most of the remaining children had experienced parental separation three or more years before being interviewed. They were described (by themselves and their parents) as having experienced some of the common early reactions to separation reported in other studies, perhaps by being silent or sad and withdrawn, or by being difficult, argumentative and miserable.[24] It should, however, be noted that at the time of interview over half the children in re-ordered families did not report problems in several of the areas measured and were doing well. The data shows clearly that, once that initial period was over, not all children reported sustained difficulties. "Things were bad but are now better" was a phrase used by both parents and children to describe this. Sometimes, however, while a study child was said to have few problems,

parents would mention another child in the family who had been acutely distressed for longer following separation. This would indicate that the inter-relationship of factors affecting children at the time of separation and divorce is complex, and can have different consequences for children in the same family. It is also consistent with the concepts explored by Rutter of "protective factors"[25] and the possibility that either protective *or* adverse factors may multiply for some children in "chain reactions".[26]

From the child's point of view, some of those who were said to be adapting well, both by their parents and themselves, nevertheless reported dissatisfaction with the arrangements for contact with their non-resident parent. They missed not having their parents together and were sad about their divorce. The level of their distress in these instances, was not always indicated by the particular outcomes measured. An Australian study by Dunlop and Burns,[27] although differing from this study by finding that there was little difference between adolescents in intact and re-ordered families, agreed that the extent to which children were upset and sad was not always reflected in negative psychological symptoms.

Conflict

The data from this study shows that the particular outcomes measured for the study children tended to be worse in intact families with high levels of conflict between the parents than in families where conflict levels were low. In agreement with nearly all other studies, the data also suggests that violence in the family has a strong association with low self-image and other poor outcomes. It is likely, moreover, that both conflict and violence are under-reported in the intact family group.

In this study, however, it was possible to compare the effects of family disruption on children in re-ordered families with those of conflict and/or violence on children living in intact families. From the multivariate analysis carried out, it appeared that the most significant factor of those examined was the re-ordering of the family – the loss of a parent on one or more occasions – rather than the presence of serious conflict or violence that was most closely associated with children's poorer outcomes as measured. This is consistent with a recent study in Oregon, which found a cumulative and linear relationship between behavioural measures in a group of boys and the number of family transitions that they had undergone.[28] In the present research, violence in the past relationship between the child's biological parents was reported by seven out of 19 resident parents in the re-disrupted families. This was the highest proportion of any sub-group, but still a minority. It was also reported by 11 of the other 57 re-ordered families and by two of the 76 intact families.

Meanwhile, it is clear from previous work that it is not the loss of a parent *per se* that appears to be associated with a poor outcome. The outcomes associated with loss of a parent by marital breakdown are different and generally more adverse in the long-term than those associated with bereavement.[29]

It is also clear that where major conflict and intra-family violence has been a feature of the marital relationship, the act of separation is often accompanied by immense relief for those who have been the victims or observers of the violence. It would follow from an understanding of the psychological processes involved that the children would experience a stability after the ending of a violent parental relationship which would enhance their well-being, at least in the short term. But the response is complex. Children's relief is also often tempered by concerns about the non-resident parent who may, or may not, have been violent to the child and may, or may not, have been a "good parent". The importance of the relationship with the non-resident parent, usually the father, has been written about extensively,[30] particularly by Richards et al., and is confirmed by the data from this study. Children expressed concerns about the non-resident parent being on their own and not having anywhere to live. Children were also concerned if contact arrangements were nebulous, and did not always find it easy to discuss the concerns for one parent with the other. Richards' study underlines the importance to the child of the biological parent, whether the family live together or not. In the Exeter Study a quarter of the children had lost touch with their non-resident parent (see Appendix 1).

Socio-economic factors

There can be no dispute that separation and divorce are almost universally accompanied by at least a period of financial difficulty, sometimes extreme, for the child's resident parent, who is usually their mother.[31] Knowing (from the authors' clinical as well as anecdotal experience) the importance of clothes, image and "street cred" to older children today, it seems reasonable to predict that, quite apart from the family stress and strain, older children would be likely to suffer poorer self-image as a result of a sudden drop in family income.

In this, as in other studies, there was clear evidence that lone parent families after divorce were very much worse off than either their matched pairs in intact families or, indeed, than in their previous, two-parent existence. The majority of lone parent families were in receipt of state benefits. Their circumstances also contrasted with the step-family group, who were not significantly worse off than their matched pairs in intact families. This, again, is consistent with previous findings. Even so, some (first-time) lone parents said they *felt* better off, even when living on reduced incomes, because of the control they had gained over their finances. Conversely, some step parents reported *feeling* badly off despite having significantly higher incomes. It should also be noted that the re-disrupted group included a number of one and two parent families who, respectively, tended to be worse off than those living in lone parent and step-families for the first time. There was, however, a higher proportion of lone parent than step families in the re-disrupted sub-group, so that the overall picture was of families whose socio-economic status was very similar to the first time lone-parent sub-group.

Judged in terms of family income, the evidence in this study that outcomes for children in (first-time) lone parent families were often close to those for children living in (first-time) step-families, could have two divergent explanations. It could be argued, as in some previous studies, that the results show how children in lone parent families might have had better outcomes than those in step-families if they had not had the additional handicap of poverty. Alternatively, it might simply be claimed that poor financial difficulties were not closely associated with poor outcomes for children when comparing these matched families.

The child's perspective

The study carried out in Exeter concentrated on obtaining children's perspectives of the outcomes of their parents' separation. It was apparent that there was a great deal of consensus between the views of children and their parents over most practical aspects of children's lives and on factual information. Where children's views and those of their parents differed markedly was over particular areas of their relationship with their non-resident parent, the acceptance of parents' new partners and how they felt generally about the divorce.

The Exeter Family Study

Children who had been part of a violent marriage were very relieved to be removed from that situation following their parent's (usually mother's) decision to end the relationship. Yet, as already mentioned, children of violent marriages had concerns about their non-resident parent, who might have had many good parenting qualities and still have been important to the child. Most of the study children were well aware of any parental conflict or violence, but many were clearly sad that the conflict had resulted in an abrupt end or alteration in their relationship with one of their parents. Indeed, several had maintained or returned to relationships with violent parents. Children's ambivalence about their non-resident parent has also been described in the study by McLoughlin and Whitefield,[32] where adolescents affected by separation and divorce expressed feelings of anger mixed with sadness. Other studies have reported the combination of children's awareness of severe parental conflict with statements that they would still have preferred their parents to stay together.[33] But even if this is recognised as a common situation where divorce follows marital violence, it is not possible to know whether the outcomes for children would have been any better (or worse) if their parents stayed together.[34]

Children who had witnessed violence between their parents could, at least, understand the reason for their separation. What this and other studies[35] have shows is that the majority of children do not understand the reason for their parent's divorce; they are given little explanation at the time and inadequate arrangements are made for continuing contact with the parent who is leaving the home. Children are left confused and bewildered, often hoping for a reconciliation for far longer than their parents imagine. Indeed, some children in the Exeter study had tried to involve their parents in joint Christmas and birthday celebrations, which proved disastrous. There were also children whose parents lived locally but who had made no plans to see them; these children found their situation particularly hard to comprehend.

Where parents had been able to overcome their differences sufficiently to make arrangements for the children without bitterness, children had accepted the drastic changes, even if they could not really understand them. They were also able to recognise the improved happiness of at least one parent. Adjustment by children could, however, be hindered by the fact that usually only one parent chooses to end the

relationship, while the other is distressed and unhappy. Children's adaptation could also be influenced by the child blaming themselves as being the cause of divorce. In this respect, studies by Wallerstein and Kelly[36] and Hetherington[37] have clearly identified the importance of the child's developmental stage at the time of separation and divorce and their psychological response to family change.

Many parents, meanwhile, said they had not been fully aware of what the consequences of separation might be for themselves or for their children. In many situations, they felt life was much improved by the ending of a failed relationship; but it was also clear that their children often regarded any improvement in a much less positive light. In fact, parents' own health and well-being was often worse after divorce,[38] and some researchers have suggested that this contributes to a reduced ability to parent responsibly and well at that time.[39] Parents who had left violent marriages generally reported fewer problems and greater relief and freedom, but in many cases, nevertheless, found caring for their children alone more stressful and tiring than they had expected.

Some resident parents expressed feelings of unexpected loneliness, as well as a sense of responsibility and concern for the health of their ex-partners.[40] Non-resident parents were, however, more likely than resident parents to say that they regretted the end of their marriage and to describe themselves as unprepared.

"For the sake of the children"

Previous studies have strongly suggested that it is parental conflict rather than their actual separation that is associated with poor outcomes for children following divorce. This has led some commentators to suggest that it is better to resolve a high conflict situation by ending the parental relationship than by allowing it to continue. This view, while not being widely promoted, has gained some credence as "accepted wisdom", and, indeed, many of the Exeter families who had divorced believed that their decision was in the best interests of their children as well as themselves. Data from this study provides some evidence that such a "justification" for divorce may be a misunderstanding of the reality. It suggests, moreover, that parental separation itself is one of the major associations with difficulties for children. What the data does not show, however, and did not set out to demonstrate, is whether the outcomes would have been better if parents in unhappy marriages had stayed together "for the sake of the children" instead of separating.

Children know that parental conflict is a not uncommon fact of family life.[41] They can not only experience unresolved conflict within their parents' marriage, but also, if there is a separation, beyond it.[42] One unspoken and unpalatable message of divorce for the child may, therefore, be that the result of conflict in families is the loss of a parent. In this study, however, as in many others, severe conflict and possible violence is not a universal feature of parental relationships before separation. An increasing number of separations occur, for example, through the partners' "incompatibility", or the wish of one parent to have a relationship with someone else. Conflict, or a higher level of conflict, may arise in those circumstances as a direct result of the decision to separate rather than being the cause of it. The present data and other studies suggest, however, that such conflict may then persist for many years after the separation.

The Exeter families also illustrate a number of reasons why children may be more closely involved in the conflict associated with and continuing after divorce. In parental conflict during marriage, the child may be able to remain on the side-lines, whereas after divorce they may be obliged to take a central role: for example, carrying messages between resident and non-resident parents who find they are unable to communicate face to face. Children in re-ordered families reported that their parents frequently "told tales" about each other, or each others' new partners. Children also sometimes felt they had to suppress telling one parent about enjoyable times they had had with the other, or had actually been asked by one parent to keep something secret from their former partner.

The present study provides clear evidence that low self-esteem is very much more common among children who have experienced their parents' separation where there is continuing conflict, poor communication or where the child is dissatisfied with the contact arrangements. It follows that separation and divorce do not necessarily reduce damaging conflict and, indeed, that as a generality the reverse may be true. In other words, the experience of most children whose parents divorce is of *increased* conflict over an extended period, with the child involved to an extent that may not have been the case while the marriage lasted.

It is also a matter of well-established fact that divorce very often results in socio-economic hardship, particularly for families where children are living with a lone parent. Some studies, such as that by Bradshaw,[43] point to poverty, and especially experience of poverty in a one parent family, as being a more important influence over children's outcomes than conflict. At all events, for children, such poverty is a significant life event that would not have occurred without their parents' separation.

In addition, children who experience their parents' divorce are likely to encounter two other potentially stressful life events:

1   Their resident parent will form a new relationship, and they will subsequently find themselves part of a step-family. In circumstances where there is relief about the departure of the non-resident parent, perhaps because of violence, this may be a welcome and positive development. But that will not apply to many children who are anxious to maintain ties with both biological parents, in spite of their separation. They may also be faced with the strain and responsibilities of having step-brothers and sisters and receiving the divided attention, real or imagined, of their parent and step-parent. For some children these new relationships will be very successful and positive, but previous research still shows that children living in step-families are more likely than those in intact or one-parent families to leave home at an earlier age for reasons associated with dissatisfaction with their family and living arrangements.[44] They are also more likely to father or bear children earlier and to enter into relationships at a younger age which are, in turn, less likely to be successful.[45]

2   Although just over a quarter of the re-ordered family children in this study had experienced multiple disruption, current trends suggest that a substantial number of children in step-families (approaching 50 per cent before the age of 16[46]) will witness the breakdown of a second relationship formed by one of their parents and the loss of another "parental" figure from their lives. In this study, this sub-group of children in re-ordered families appeared to fare particularly badly and were very much more likely to experience adverse outcomes, than other children.

Use of services

The study looked at divorce settlements and the use that families made of support and legal services. As the study was carried out before the effects of the Children Act, most decisions had been made by parents using a particularly adversarial approach. Mothers were much more likely than fathers to have been granted sole custody, to have been awarded some maintenance, and to have made some provision for the child to see the non-resident parent (either as a defined or an undefined agreement). Where there had been marital violence, families often felt that there had been inadequate recognition of their difficulties, and that they had not received the support necessary to provide protection for parent and child, or contact arrangements that felt safe.[47]

Relate had provided counselling and support for a minority of parents, but once separation had occurred it appeared there were few support services available to parents that did not label them as either "patients" or "clients". Child-centred mediation services – provided "in court" by the Probation Service, or independently, were available in Exeter at the time of the study, but only a minority of the study group parents had used them. However, comprehensive family mediation concerned with property agreements as well as arrangements for children was not, at that time, available.[48] Families were evidently confused about the role of the probation service,[49] but apart from those that had been referred for a Court Welfare Officer's report, no parents suggested that their children's views had been adequately taken into account during divorce proceedings.

Parents in intact families acknowledged the support that they gave to each other and that they received, in most cases, from extended family members, particularly grandparents. Grandparents were evidently an important source of continuity and support to children, especially if they lived locally.[50] In both the intact and re-ordered families, maternal grandparents were most often recognised as providing this support. Indeed, in step-families it seemed that, even after re-partnering, many parents were more likely to seek support from their relatives than from their new partners. However, most children in re-disrupted families had either lost or significantly reduced their contact with grandparents. Both children and parents in re-partnered families, meanwhile, said they found step-parents were supportive to children, although recent research suggests that these relationships are sometimes prone to be emotionally "thin" and unenduring[347].

Children in re-ordered families were more likely to have friends whose parents were separated and to whom they could talk freely about events at home – even when they were not always able to talk to family members. Children had also sometimes talked about family problems to their teachers at school, an important avenue of support for children under stress.[51] In contrast with some studies that suggested schools might unfairly "label" children from "broken homes",[52] Exeter schools were found to be very careful about confidentiality. It appeared, however, that teachers tended to under-estimate the effects of family change on the child's performance and well-being. They were often confused about their roles in supporting children and also about their relationship with non-resident parents. As a result, it seemed they were unable to provide children with systematic support.[53]

Within the small group of children referred for acute or chronic behavioural problems, most had valued an opportunity to talk to someone who was "not a parent", although a minority had been unable to co-operate or make use of the service offered. Parents expressed concern that help was invariably only available as a therapeutic intervention for their children; they would have preferred more a informal and accessible service.

All the study families had, meanwhile, needed to seek outside help at various times when a problem arose. But re-ordered families were much more likely to have needed assistance than intact families. Family doctors, family lawyers, and schools were generally considered to be supportive by parents who had been through separation and divorce. However, they also identified a lack of readily available advice and information when they were at their most confused in the early stages of separation. They would have appreciated more information regarding the divorce process and its effects as well as advice on how to re-organise their finances and housing, and arrange contact with the non-resident parent for their children .

In summary

The findings from this pilot study indicate that although *most* children do not exhibit acute difficulties beyond the initial stage of family breakdown *a significant minority* of children encounter long-term problems. Compared with their matched pairs in intact families, children who had experienced their parents' divorce were more likely to report problems in key areas of their lives, including psychosomatic disorders, difficulties with school work and a low sense of self-esteem. They were more likely to feel confused and uninvolved in arrangements about their future and to have lasting feelings of concern about both their resident and non-resident parents. Parental conflict and financial difficulties are clearly important features of family reorganisation that are associated with adverse outcomes for children. However, in this study it appeared that a more important adverse factor was the loss of a parent and the consequences, which included the risk that history would repeat itself with the breakdown of subsequent parental relationships.

1   This has been explored in a number of studies of marriage including those of Mansfield, P. & Collard, J. (1988); McRae S. (1993); Furstenberg, F.F. et al. (1984).

2   Recent reviews have included those by Hodges, W.F. (1986), Pasley, K. & Ihinger-Tallman, M. (1987) Emery, R.E. (1988); Hetherington, E.M. and Camara, K.A. (1988). Amato, P. & Bruce, K. (1991) have published a meta-analysis of 92 studies.

3   Cherlin, A.J. et al. (1991).

4   Reported by Furstenberg, F.F. and colleagues (1983, 1984, 1985), whose studies look at children's lives post-divorce and in remarried families.

5   Wadsworth, M. & Maclean, M. (1986) have looked at the lives of those children who were part of the 1946 birth cohort study, and have assessed long term outcomes.

6   See, for example, Ferri, E. et al. (1993); Kiernan, K. et al. (1991).

7   Fergusson, D.M. et al. (1986). A study on a birth cohort of twelve hundred New Zealand children, born in 1980.

8   Rutter, M. (1976); Rutter, M. (1989a,b).

9   See Wadsworth, M.E. (1991), who discusses the long term effects of divorce including the hightened chances of the child of divorced parents repeating the pattern. See also Hetherington, E.M. et al. (1992); Wallerstein, J. et al. (1989); Quinton, D. & Rutter, M. (1988) on inter-generational links.

10 Wallerstein, J. & Kelly, J.B. (1980); Kelly, J.B. (1981); Wallerstein, J. (1984); Wallerstein, J. et al. (1988).

11 Hetherington, E.M. et al. (1979, 1982); Hetherington, E.M. et al. (1992).

12 Block, J.H. et al. (1986) This study of children over time included data collected pre-divorce and post-divorce about childrens outcomes.

13 Guidubaldi, J. et al. (1984). See also Appendix 1.

14 Peterson, J. & Zill, N. (1986).

15 Capaldi, D.M. & Patterson, G.R. (1991).

16 McLoughlin, D. & Whitfield, R.R. (1984). See also Appendix 1.

17 Jenkins, J.M. & Smith, M.A. (1990).

18 Rutter, M. (1989); Hetherington, E.M. et al. (1992); Peterson, J. & Zill, N. (1986); Bradshaw, J. (1991); Jenkins, J.M. & Smith, M.A. (1990).

19 Amato, P. & Bruce, K. (1991); Cherlin, A.J. & Furstenberg, F.F. (1986); Kiernan, K. & Chase-Lansdale (1991).

20 Especially for boys. See Cherlin, A.J. et al. (1991); Block, J.H. et al. (1986).

21 Hodges, W.F. (1986). See also reviews by Pasley, K. & Ihinger-Tallman, M. (1987) and the Amato, P. & Bruce, K. (1991) meta-analysis. The general consensus being that associations are complex concerning the effect of adverse life events on children of divorce and that conflict can begin at the time of divorce.

22 These included schools in both the state and independent sectors.

23 For example Hetherington, E.M. et al. (1985); Wallerstein, J. and Kelly, J.B. (1980).

24 See Amato, P. & Bruce, K. (1991).

25 Rutter, M. (1989). This paper explores the child's ability to resist adverse life factors.

26 Reported by Goodyer (1990, 1991) in studies carried out to look at the possible link between clinical symptoms and the child's experience of adverse life events.

27 Dunlop, R. & Burns, A. (1983).

28 Capaldi, D.M. & Patterson, G.R. (1991).

29 Wallerstein, J. & Kelly, J.B. (1980) give an excellent account of the probable qualitative differences of these two situations and their psychological impact. Various cohort studies confirm the quantative differences in effects, e.g. Kiernan, K. (1992); Maclean, M. & Wadsworth, M.E. (1988); Kuh, D. & Maclean, M. (1990).The historical comparison between the present-day prevalence of divorce and the higher levels of parental bereavement a century ago when step-parents were "stepping in" to take the place of a dead parent is discussed in Burgoyne, J. & Clark, D. (1984).

30 Richards, M.P. (1987, 1982). These papers discuss the conflicting roles of the resident and non-resident parent and the child in the child's view of family after divorce.

31 Bradshaw, J. & Millar, J. (1991); Eekelaar, J. & Maclean, M. (1986); Maclean, M. & Eekelaar, J. (1983).

32 McLoughlin, D. & Whitefield (1984).

33 Mitchell, A. (1985); Walzak, Y. & Burns, A. (1984); Wallerstein, J. & Kelly, J.B. (1980). Qualitative data on children's feelings about separation from and contact with their non-resident parents are described in some cases by children years after the event.

34 In a review of literature by Hodges, W.F. (1986), he comments on a study by Johnson, A.J.R., Campbell, L.E.G. & Mayes, S.S. (1985), which suggests that children may have a role in keeping conflict between parents going, so that parents will communicate. This Hodges describes as "child instigated conflict".

35 Walzak, Y. & Burns, A. (1984); Mitchell, A. (1985); Hetherington, E.M. (1986). See also Appendix 1.

36 Wallerstein, J. & Kelly, J.B. (1980).

37 Hetherington, E.M. (1987).

38 See also Wadsworth, M.E. (1987); Chester, R. (1973).

39 Hetherington, E.M. et al. (1992); Wallerstein, J. & Kelly, J.B. (1980); Dominian, J. et al. (1991).

40 As discussed by Cherlin, A.J. (1981) and Weiss, R. (1975).

41 Ahrons, S.C.R. & Rogers, R. (1987); Jenkins, J.M. & Smith, M.A. (1991).

42 Elliot, J. & Richards, M.P. (1991).

43 Bradshaw, J. (1991); Burghes (1993).

44 Visher, E.B. & Visher, J.S. (1987); Furstenberg, F.F. et al. (1984); Smith, M.A. & Robertson (1993); Santrock, J.W. & Sitterle, K. (1987); Kiernan, K. (1992).

45 Wadsworth, M.E. et al. (1986); Ferri (1976); Kiernan, K. (1992).

46 Bumpass, L. (1984).

47 See also Yellot, A. (1990); Furstenberg, F.F. et al. (1983); Pearson, J. (1992).

48 See Walker et al. (1994) for evidence that comprehensive mediation may place less stress on children by increasing the likelihood of their parents reaching an agreement.

49 See also Hodges, W.F. (1986); Eekalaar, J. and McLean, M. (1986); Eekelaar, J. (1991).

50 As also found by Willmott, P (1986).

51 Cherlin, A.J. (1978) and other studies discussed in Pasley, K. & Ihinger -Tallman, M. (1987).

52 See Wallerstein, J. & Kelly, J.B. (1980).

53 For example, Santrok, J. & Tracey, R.L. (1978); Ourth, et al. (1982); Shinn (1978).

54 See also Clark, D. et al. (1989), which looks at the support levels provided for children who have experienced divorce in a sample of first and high schools.

Recommendations

Context

The context in which we make our recommendations as a result of the findings of this study are well known to research workers, professionals, policy makers, politicians and, most importantly, to members of society –both adults and children – and particularly to those who have themselves experienced family breakdown.

This context (reviewed and referenced in the introduction and discussion sections) includes:

- Family reorganisation resulting from the breakdown of "permanent" relationships between parents, which is now such a common event that it must be considered to be a normal part of family experience. Every year over 150,000 children under the age of 16 are involved in the breakdown of marriages, although this figure may grossly underestimate the total number involved in family reorganisation as one in five children (another 120,000 per year) are born outside marriage and the breakdown of cohabiting arrangements is at least as frequent as the breakdown of marriage.

- There is no disagreement that children involved in such family reorganisation are disadvantaged in a number of ways:

  - poorer self-esteem.

  - more difficulties in their daily lives with health, school performance, friendships and behaviour.

  - increased long term likelihood of lower socio-economic grouping, associated with reduced educational and vocational qualifications.

  - increased likelihood of early and shorter-lasting personal relationships with sexual partners, with the associated increased risk of birth outside marriage and breakdown of their own marriages.

However, these adverse outcomes are not universal, but apply to groups of children whose experiences are very varied.

It is clear that the reasons for marital breakdown, and its consequences are extremely diverse, ranging from the break-up of an extremely violent relationship where all the family members may have lived in fear of one member (and where the change in family life is a relief to the children), to the breakdown of a marriage which, from external viewpoints (including the children's viewpoint), was a satisfactory and happy relationship. This and other variables (such as the actual process of the breakdown of the relationship, the arrangements made for access and contact between the children and their parents, the children's own personalities, and other factors in the children's lives which might either exacerbate or ameliorate the effects) mean that some children will experience severe adverse outcomes but that others will fare better on measures of outcome than some children in intact families, particularly those where there is significant parental conflict.

There is some disagreement about the causes of the disadvantage experienced by children in reorganised families, but it is clearly mediated to some extent by the effects of parental conflict both during and after the breakdown of permanent relationships, and by the financial consequences of family breakdown. The findings of this study suggest that the most important association with these effects is the loss of parenting figures from the child's life. This is particularly apparent in those children who have experienced multiple disruption. We do not have any data on the effects of single parenthood from birth so that it is as stated –the loss of a parent rather than their absence – that has been investigated.

There is widespread concern about the effects of family reorganisation in our society as a whole, and general agreement that although the lives of some parents in some situations have been improved, the needs of the present generation of children are not being met, and that the results of this failure may have adverse long term effects on society itself. The concern of government is seen by some to be a purely fiscal one, but whatever the motivation, the response of policy-makers has been to try to maintain the responsibilities of parents for their children beyond divorce, and, most recently, to address the issues of divorce itself in an attempt to reduce the adverse effects on children. Those who provide family support are concerned by the dearth of services to encourage that responsibility, and parents in the study said that the few available services were inaccessible and hard to find.

The Children Act (1989) strongly underlines and reinforces parental responsibility to and for the children of a couple's relationship both during and after marriage. The Child Support Act (implemented in 1993) extends the natural parent's financial responsibility to the children of all relationships in which both parents can be identified. The Lord Chancellor's 1993 Green Paper *Looking to the Future. Mediation and the Grounds for Divorce* is a clear attempt to reduce the adversarial aspects of divorce proceedings by changing the grounds for divorce and by introducing mediation services. The proposed changes in grounds for divorce would remove the need for "fault-based" divorce (with the possibility of contrived and/or agreed allegations) for those seeking early divorce, but would prevent divorce in less than 12 months. The introduction of widespread mediation is seen to be a way of ensuring careful consideration by both parents and of reducing the adversarial element of divorce.

In this study, as in others, all parents wished to minimise difficulties for their children, recognising them to be innocent parties; the vast majority of parents would have been willing to try to alter their behaviour to achieve this end if they had been aware of alternative steps they could take. Before their separation, however, parents often poorly informed in a number of critical areas. They are often unaware of the financial costs and personal implications of the divorce itself, with the need to establish fault (with associated recriminations) if they wish to divorce in less than two years. They often feel that their children, like themselves, will be relieved at the resolution of difficult personal relationships by separation. They are unaware of the likely strength of the attachment that their children would retain for their non-resident parent, and of the statistical likelihood of reduced life chances for those children in both the short and long term. Non-resident parents often regretted their decision to separate, feeling much more isolated, particularly from the day-to-day lives of their children, than they had anticipated, while some resident parents found sole responsibility for their children a greater problem than expected. Parents also did not always acknowledge the difficulties faced by each other at the end of the relationship (especially by the "guilty party").

Minimising the adverse effects for children

There are a number of ways in which we believe that parents could reduce the adverse outcomes for their children, remembering that parents themselves say that their own ability to make good decisions can be affected by the pain and confusion of separation:

- It is clearly important for children that they are fully informed at a level appropriate to their own development of the events that occur, and that parents are honest with their children about the fact that changes are going to take place. If the parents could to talk to their children together, it would give the children a much more accurate appreciation of what was happening and, most importantly, they could be prepared for future changes, rather than finding out subsequently with the inevitable feeling that they had been deceived. Parents may need to remember that children may never understand their parent's actions.

- Disagreements are a very common consequence of separation, and it is unreasonable to expect that the arrangements for contact will be without difficulty for the parents. However, it ought to be possible for parents, given an understanding of the consequences for their children, to keep such disagreements out of the day-to-day concerns of their children and, in particular, not to make demands of the children to act as peace- or war-makers with the other parent. An understanding by both parents that their roles towards their children must, of necessity, change with the change in residence, would enable both parents to fulfil those roles better, and with less friction than is the case when both have unreal expectations of their own and/or the other's roles.

- Parents should try to appreciate that, in many cases, the child may not have cause to be in conflict with the non-resident parent; that the parent's and the children's views of the other parent can, and possibly should, be quite different, and that the facility of contact is an important marker for good outcomes, which would:

  – Allow the children to maintain good quality contact with both parents from an early stage after separation at a level and timing of their own choosing, which means not being forced into regular contact that they do not want and not being prevented from contact by artificial difficulties raised by their parents as part of the conflict resolution between themselves.

– Prevent parents having to justify their position to the child, for example, by exaggeration of their ex-partner's misdemeanours or "bad" behaviour.

– Facilitate the maintenance of contact between the child and other important relatives, particularly grandparents.

– Enable the introduction of new parent figures into the child's life without the need for the other parent to undermine that relationship.

• Knowledge by parents of the fact that the reaction of their children may be unexpectedly severe and lead to changes of behaviour presenting themselves as either internalised or externalised difficulties, would enable them to seek earlier counselling and help for the children if this was known to be available.

The above will strike the reader as a catalogue of unattainable and utopian expectations, but is included to illustrate that a great deal is known of ways in which children could be helped to survive the break-up of their parents. Can policy-makers and service providers do anything to make the process by which parents handle family breakdown less damaging to children?

Changes in policy and practice

There is little doubt in the authors minds that the Lord Chancellor's proposals and both of the Acts of Parliament referred to above are framed in such a way as to take many of the above requirements into account and to assist parents and service providers in keeping the needs of children at the centre of divorce arrangements. The Children Act very positively emphasises the continuing responsibilities of parents but stresses that decision-making must be based on the needs of the child. The Child Support Act again emphasises the responsibilities of non-resident parents, though in a way that is often very unwelcome to the non-resident parent and may actually exacerbate difficulties between parents. Both these Acts, however, provide a basis for clear educational initiatives for both adults and children in school, which will emphasise the continuing responsibilities of parenthood and

which have already been shown to have some beneficial effects. The increasing dilemma is whether to accept that there is a limit to the way in which family law can and should influence family relationships.

Mediation and conciliation

The Lord Chancellor's Green Paper envisages offering mediation as a positive option and in preference, where ever possible, to individual representation by lawyers for all divorcing couples. It puts an emphasis on:

• The need to inform parents fully of the financial and social consequences of their decision.

• The need to give parents the opportunity for reconciliation early in the process of divorce proceedings.

Very few of the parents in this study were even aware of conciliation and mediation services and only four couples had used them; only 14 couples had approached Relate prior to their decision to separate. The evidence so far available is that if mediation is to be effective it needs to be highly professional, and decisions need to be at least ratified by lawyers, if they are not actually involved in the conciliation process, as in the Family Mediators Association model and in some of the other pilot comprehensive mediation initiatives evaluated by Walker et al.[1] Given this quality of service there is evidence that mediation enables parents to communicate more effectively and to be better informed about the ways in which they can achieve their aim of minimising adverse effects on their children.

The rationale is that decisions made by parents themselves, with the help of mediators, may last longer than adjudicated ones. We welcome the emphasis on mediation in the Green Paper but, like many other respondents to the consultation, we are concerned about the lack of clarity in relation to the background and additional training envisaged for mediators, and indeed the lack of any statement about the methods of mediation to be adopted. There is also concern about how existing services (e.g. the court welfare service and Children Act provision) can be linked to the "mediation path" if parents choose that route.

We recommend that changes to the current arrangements should enable high quality mediation to be available to all divorcing couples emphasising the potential advantages of this process in helping them to keep the needs of their children at the forefront of their negotiations. For this to happen there will have

to be national initiatives including:

- Some incentive for lawyers to encourage referral to mediation.

- The adoption of agreed standards for mediation and the training of appropriate professionals.

- Training of people who already have relevant professional qualifications and/or experience to act as mediators. Continued and expanded training of lawyers as conciliators, advisers to conciliators, "checkers of mediated agreements", or all three of these roles will be essential. The importance of legal advice to clarify issues of abuse and domestic violence need to be linked into the proposed systems for parents who need it.[2]

No fault divorce

The same Green Paper introduces the concept of "no fault" divorce with the stated aim of reducing the adversarial nature of many divorces (75 per cent are fault-based and a further small percentage remain contested at the end of 5 years separation). The Green Paper emphasises that, although this measure will reduce the time taken to achieve no fault divorce from 2 or 5 (contested separation) years, it will actually increase the time for most divorces (median of 6 months for the 75 per cent fault-based decisions) to a 1 year minimum, except under possible particular circumstances. There are implications in terms of how marriage as a legal contract will be viewed. Critics of the Green Paper are concerned that removing the "fault" ground will lighten the weight of parental responsibility.

Emphasis on a serious attempt at reconciliation at an early stage of the process, to underwrite the importance of marriage at an early stage, is written in to the Green Paper as a counterbalance to the removal of the fault-based grounds.

We therefore recommend that:

- A greater emphasis be placed on an early opportunity for parents to consider and explore reconciliation as an alternative to proceeding with divorce.

- "No fault" divorce by means of a proper process of mediation be introduced as an alternative to 2 years separation, with agreement as grounds for divorce, rather than replacement of other grounds.

- Inclusion of a mechanism to enable children to receive advice and support independently of their parents, not necessarily on an individual basis.

We believe that these measures would allow for the exploration and development of the proposals without irrevocable commitment to a radical change in the law at this stage, while the balance between parental responsibility and parental freedom is further explored.

Professional education

In addition to the proposals for education inherent in the extension of mediation, there is evidence from this study that parents and children need better access to professionals who are well placed to help them, rather than the services currently available. Parents report having sought advice from GPs who, though sympathetic and supportive, did not usually direct them to services that might encourage attempts at reconciliation at an early stage, or to non-adversarial services to assist in the management of their separation. Children and parents recognised the need for children to have access to independent counselling to assist them in dealing with the issues that arise both at home and at school, and regretted that such services were available only in crisis situations. This necessitated children being referred to a therapeutic service for support, from which point they felt they had been labelled.

We recommend that courses are set up to inform relevant professionals, particularly primary health care staff and teachers, of the existence of, and the referral arrangements for, such services, emphasising their potential importance in reducing adverse outcomes for children.

General education

Other studies demonstrate widespread ignorance and false expectations of marriage[3] and men and women's differing approaches to parenthood at a time when an understanding of these issues, at a level that would be useful in everyday life, seems ever more important. Previously unchallenged concepts and expectations of marriage have been radically altered by social, economic and legal influences.

Young people and adults, though often having traditional aspirations for a stable nuclear family, are sometimes unable to fulfil their expectations in the face of other pressures. It is acknowledged that concepts of what constitutes "family" have altered radically in practice, and it is inappropriate for policy-makers to cling to the nuclear family as the only acceptable environment in which to raise children. However, research has also shown that the current alternatives for couples already in permanent relationships can also carry significant financial, legal and emotional risks for the couple themselves, as well as for their children. Other research has shown that children have fewer problems in low conflict, stable family groups; these findings are supported by this study. Despite this, a very large number of children and young adults have no clear model on which to base their own relationships, as their experience of marriage is of dispute, separation and loss of parents from their lives.

An examination of the complexity of human relationships and family life within the framework of social and philosophical issues is part of the core educational curriculum in many European countries, though not in Britain. The findings of this study emphasise the importance of the school environment, not only as a place where children may exhibit difficulties associated with experiences outside school, but also as an arena for support.

We recommend that the core educational curriculum for all children should be adapted to include components that address social and philosophical issues of modern life with particular reference to issues of personal relationships and family life.

An important part of this curriculum would be the acknowledgement of the pluralistic nature of modern life and the exploration of the many forms of family in which children find themselves. Normalisation of this experience, with recognition that families commonly do not have the traditional form that children still believe to be the norm, would enable teachers and others to address these issues. This would allow children to feel better about themselves so that the resulting improvement in self-image might break the cycle of under-achievement that affects many of these children.

1   Walker et al. (1989) Cost and *Effectiveness of Family Conciliation*. Lord Chancellor's Department (London)

2   Hestor, M. & Radford, L. (1992)

3   Mansfield, P. & Collard, J. (1988)

Previous Research

"Children's development cannot be explained solely in terms of their environment and what other people do to them."[1]

Research about families and children has always been closely linked to the social, financial and legal influences on the nature of the family, its changing structure and the interaction of social and economic policy on family life.[2]

Different studies have focused on the wider social implications of the changing nature of families, the economic consequences and the role of the law and families.

Research into families and children and the effects of separation and divorce on the child, parents and extended family networks have shown that the relationships are complex. Studies have underlined several important factors that seem to be present in situations that can either cause children long term harm or present children with difficulty. These are:

- The effect of family conflict, either during marriage or after the marriage has ended.

- The changing economic circumstances experienced by families at the time of separation and divorce.

- Geographical relocation, which can take place when families break down.

- The child's relationship with both parents.

- Parental remarriage.

- The resident parent's psychological adjustment to multiple life stresses.[3]

Longitudinal studies carried out in the USA,[4] analysis of cohort studies in the UK (Ferri;[5] Wadsworth et al.;[6] Kiernan et al.[7]) and New Zealand (Fergusson and Dimond[8]) and work done by Furstenberg and Allison,[9] has looked at the long term effects of separation and divorce on children. Children whose parents have divorced are more likely to suffer problems at school, with their health, friendships, behaviour.[10] Their long term chances of tertiary education, employment, and of getting divorced themselves[11] are also more negatively affected by separation and

divorce.[12] Longitudinal studies have found that children's outcomes are less affected by the loss of a parent through death rather than parental divorce.[13]

Research has also looked at the effects on parental health of separation and divorce, particularly in the longitudinal studies carried out by Hetherington and Cox,[14] Chester,[15] Wadsworth et al.[16] and Dominian.[17]

Several kinds of studies have been undertaken to look into the effects of separation and divorce on children:

1 *Longitudinal studies.*

2 *Cohort studies* (e.g. those carried out in the USA on a national collection of children's data by Furstenberg[18] and in the UK by the 1946 Birth Cohort study and the 1958 National Child Development study, which began as a Perinatal Death study. Work has been done on these studies by Wadsworth et al.,[19] Kuh and MacLean,[20] Kiernan et al.[21] and Ferri[22]).

3 *Clinical studies* (e.g. Wallerstein and Kelly[23] and Kalter[24] in the USA, and studies in the UK by Rutter[25] and Goodyer[26]).

4 *Empirical studies*, a wide range of which has looked at different aspects of the child's response to separation and divorce and to living in different family groups (e.g. Guidubaldi et al.;[27] Capaldi;[28] Kalter.[29] Also the studies reviewed by Emery[30] and the Amato meta-analysis[31]).

Most of the major studies carried out in the past 30 years have been included in reviews by Amato,[32] Emery[33] and Pasley Ihinger-Tallman.[34] The Emery review and the Amato meta-analysis have concentrated on the complex association of different life events which can negatively affect childrens' outcomes. The Pasley and Ihinger-Tallman[35] review has concentrated on the complexities of remarriage. Fewer studies have looked at the effect of multiple disruption; those that have include Ferri,[36] Bumpass et al.,[37] Peterson et al.,[38] Capaldi[39] and Furstenberg et al.[40]

Research into the changing structure of families has tended to concentrate mainly on the differences between children living in intact and re-ordered families and of the experience of children living in lone parent families.[41] There is a growing literature of research looking at the child's experience of family life prior to divorce,[42] and at the different groups in which children live after separation and divorce.

One of the findings from the Amato analysis was that methodologically robust studies found smaller differences between intact and re-ordered groups, whereas methodologically less satisfactory studies sometimes found bigger differences. This statement has been tempered by the fact that studies are beginning to look at the different kinds of family groups formed after separation and divorce, rather than look globally at "re-ordered families". Studies of lone parents, re-married and multi-disrupted families have found that children may experience more problems in some groups than in others.

In some instances, studies found that family type appears to account for the findings (e.g. Capaldi et al.,[43] who found that children are particularly vulnerable to the "cumulative and linear effect" of family problems according to the number of family transitions experienced).

Criticism has been made in reviews of the literature (e.g. by Hodges,[44] Emery[45]) that the majority of studies, particularly the more empirical or clinical studies, have been based on middle class white family groups, rather than taking a broader look across social classes. Studies carried out by Capaldi et al.[46] and Furstenberg et al.,[47] have addressed this.

Apart from the longitudinal studies, most studies looking at families and children have tended to be small, which makes it difficult to draw conclusions. Almost all differences between various groups of children are small and it is difficult to relate problems to one particular event or circumstance; findings indicate that it is more likely to be a complex web of events.

With separation and divorce it is almost impossible to separate out causal factors because the kind of life events experienced by parents and children, and the changes associated with family breakdown, are very complex and are affected by other factors, such as the child's age, sex and relationship with their parents.

Qualitative studies to obtain the views of children have been undertaken in the UK by Walzack and Burns,[48] and in the USA by Burgoyne et al.[49] Qualitative and longitudinal studies by Wallerstein and Kelly[50] and other work by Furstenberg et al.[51] and Amato,[52] record the child's view. In Australia, Dunlop and Burns[53] have studied the views of a sample of adolescents and, in the UK, the views of children and adolescents have been recorded in a qualitative study by Mitchell.[54]

Five main areas of research are highlighted by most major longitudinal studies as being important in the complex interactions between the child and the family:

1 Parent loss (or partial loss).

2 Socio-economic factors.

3 Inter-parental conflict.

4 Remarriage.

5 Psychological adjustment of resident parent.

Other important elements have been highlighted by particular studies, such as the age of the child at the time of separation (Wallerstein and Kelly[55]), the sex of the child in relation to the custodial parent (Hetherington et al.[56]) and the effects of time following divorce (Wadsworth et al.5[7]). There is an increasing attempt to address what is described by Schaffer[58] as the fact of adaptability: *"What can be done to help children cope with the consequences of adversity?"*

Parent loss

The attachment and loss theory explored by Bowlby in the 1950s was largely discounted by studies carried out during the 1960s and 1970s, which seemed to indicate that replacement parental figures for children, if they were warm and supportive, meant that the mother and father role, particularly the mother's role and the attachment process for children, was not all important.

There has always been some support for the importance to the child of the biological parents[59] and Bowlby's theories have been expounded more recently by Robert Karen in the USA in an article published in *Atlantic Monthly* in 1990 and, more recently, in a book published in 1994, which also describes the work done by Ainsworth in the UK, placing the attachment theory in a wider context.

Bowlby's[60] theory developed in later work suggests that: *"Because we have lost the abundance of secondary attachment figures the attachment to a parental figure has become more important to children and consequently, the loss."* Researchers have been slow to look at the link between the attachment and parental loss theory and the effects of separation and divorce on children, but studies have begun to examine the theory in terms of the child's continuing relationship with a non-resident parent. Richards[61] puts forward the view that the child's concept of "family" would almost always include both biological parents, and that "families" will not necessarily live together but are defined not by residence but by members belonging to the family network.

As with any attempts to look at life events and children, causative factors are complex, not least because of the "reverse causation" effect whereby children can have an influence on their own parents' relationship. Some children are more difficult to manage than others and, rather than being solely the victims of parental difficulties, in some conflictual situations the child may have contributed towards them.[62]

Most resident parents are mothers and studies have shown that during the time of family breakdown, because of their own difficulties, the resident parent may have less time to nurture the child[63] so that parental loss will include the loss incurred from reduced parenting by the resident parent. Resident, single parents may also be obliged to return to work, which will make that parent less available to the child.

Studies by Hetherington et al.,[64] Wadsworth et al.,[65] Wallerstein and Kelly,[66] and other studies carried out in the USA, have shown that girls adapt better than boys to living with their mothers. Girls' behaviour at the time of separation and divorce may be more introspective and quiet than boys', but while boys can be more outgoing, noisy and difficult, they may adapt less well, even over time, to living with their mothers.

There are fewer "father custody" cases where boys appear to adapt more easily than girls.[67] Children of the same sex as their resident parent may be better adjusted, more socially competent and happier with living arrangements, and boys living with their father show less tendency towards delinquency than children living with the opposite sex parent.

Lone parent families often have a low socio-economic status and the link between the mother's ability to cope and socio-economic difficulties is discussed in several longitudinal studies in the Emery review.[45] Mothers can feel depressed and cut-off from family and friendship networks, and those with more severe socio-economic difficulties have the greatest problems.

Relationship with the non-resident parent

Longitudinal studies have shown the importance of contact for the child with their non-resident parent. Wallerstein and Kelly[68] and Hetherington et al.[69] have looked at the continuity or otherwise of contact. The quality and nature of contact can also have important implications for the child. The non-resident parent may not in fact be called upon to "parent the child post-divorce", as discussed in Hodges review, and "non-resident parenting may be a leisure time activity" (Pasley et al.).[70]

The resident parent may be carrying out all of the accepted parental duties and responsibilities towards the child, i.e. affection, support, security, discipline and guidance, and the non-resident parent may just be "providing entertainment". This is not always the case and may not be true of all relationships. In a study on non-resident parenting carried out by Furstenberg and Nord,[71] children and their resident parent were asked to record all the members of their family; even children with low levels of contact with their non-resident parent were ten times more likely to include this parent as a member of their family than their resident parent was. Not all studies showed that frequency of contact was linked to better adjustment. Some found that frequent contact was linked to greater aggression.[72] Others (e.g. Wallerstein and Kelly[73] and Hetherington[74]) did associate more frequent contact with better adjustment.

The importance of biological parents in the eyes of children is emphasised by Richards,[75] whose work shows its importance even when contact with the non-resident parent is reduced by remarriage of the resident parent and the child is presented with new conflicts of loyalties and new relationships to develop.[76]

Extended family networks

When families separate, studies have shown that children and parents can lose touch with and receive less support from grandparents, particularly the non-resident parent grandparents. From the grandparents' point of view, not only do they have infrequent or no contact with grandchildren, but they also may lose the care and support they need in return.[77] Grandparents of new relationships have been shown to be supportive to children of new partners, but this support may not be long-lasting.[78] The making and breaking of intergenerational bonds is discussed by Cherlin.[79]

Socio-economic factors

"Income decline rather than absolute income levels may be a better indication of the family's financial status."

The effects of the reduction in financial status on children and economic difficulties faced by parents after separation and divorce, have been shown in some studies to be the most important outcome of marital breakdown.[80] In almost all situations marital breakdown results in a poorer socio-economic background for both parent and child. Living in a lone parent household is associated with lower socio-economic status, while the Jacobs and Furstenberg study[81] showed that "always married" and "re-married families" had similar financial status.

The economic effects of divorce can themselves set into motion a series of changes that can challenge children's coping resources, such as moving house, changing schools and making new friends. Kalter's papers (1987, 1989)[82] discuss the effects of the process of divorce on children and the associated life stresses, which can accumulate over time and can add to the child's inability to adapt: *"Unfolding post- divorce processes are tantamount to laying multiple land-mines in the path of child development"*.

Should a single parent wish to work, the child may spend more time in child care settings; parents may also be more pre-occupied with finance and contact arrangements and can have less energy for parenting.[83] Bradshaw's study[84] assesses the effects of poverty on lone parent families and the levels of maintenance paid to resident parents. Although 29 per cent of his study group received maintenance payments, actual sums paid were low. Step-families were more successful in obtaining maintenance payments. Although only 29 per cent of absent parents were paying maintenance, 57 per cent did have contact with their children, which does not seem to support the view that maintenance and contact are linked.

This socio-economic disadvantage appears to be cross-generational, according to longitudinal studies carried out so far.[85] It not only affects the child's quality of living in the years immediately following divorce but, because of lack of opportunity for entry into higher education, their economic futures may also be jeopardised. However, socio-economic factors as an influence on outcomes (as emphasised by reviews of studies by Amato et al.;[86] Hodges;[87] Emery[88]) are closely linked with whether the child remains in a lone parent family, whether their parents remarry and the effects of that remarriage on their future life chances, or whether they experience multiple disruption.

In Australia, Dunlop and Burns[89] found that the material circumstances of children did not seem to be of first importance in predicting or affecting outcomes; there was little difference between the outcome of adolescents in this study between children whose parents had divorced and children whose parents who had remained together.

In a study by Hodges,[90] it was shown that limited financial resources were linked to problems of children after divorce but not to problems shown by children in intact families. The Amato meta-analysis[91] also looks at a study done by Guidubaldi,[92] which allowed for differences in income between intact and re-ordered families. Where income was the same, children in re-ordered families continued to score below children in intact families. Amato comments that: *"This indicates the economic disadvantage cannot be the sole explanation for the impact of divorce on children."*

Another study discussed in the Amato meta-analysis looks at whether there are fewer financial problems for children in father-custody families rather than mother-custody families, because fathers usually earn more than mothers. Studies which have looked at this include the Australian study by Dunlop and Burns[93] and Peterson and Zill.[94] (These are small studies because fewer children lived with their fathers than with their mothers.)

However, the effects of socio-economic deprivation linked to mother- or father-custody is somewhat confused by the fact that children's outcomes can vary according to whether a child lives with the same sex parent or otherwise. Studies carried out by Camara and Resnick[95] and Santrock and Warshak[96] found significant differences between girls living with their mothers and boys living with their fathers, so that the economic effect will also be linked to a parental absence effect. (This effect of children living with parents of the same sex has been looked at by studies carried out by Hetherington[97] and also is discussed by Wallerstein and Kelly.[98])

Inter-parental conflict

"Staying together for the sake of the children."

"Whether accommodation to the interests of adults means that the family is not serving the needs of the children remains to be confirmed."[9]

There has been considerable interest in research which has shown that children in disharmonious homes, whether intact or re-ordered families, have more problems than children in low conflict homes (Jenkins and Smith;[100] Dunlop and Burns;[101] Chase-Lansdale et al.[102]).

Longitudinal studies show that poor adaption to the conflict within a marriage is often apparent before the separation, and problems for the children may simply be a result of that pre-divorce conflict.[103] Studies by Kurdek, Blisk and Seisky[104] and Parish and Wigle[105] found that differences between children who had experienced separation and divorce and children in intact families lessened over time. Studies by Hetherington,[106] Wadsworth[107] and Kelly,[108] have also suggested a link with decreased conflict.

After divorce, if parents can make good plans for the child and reduce inter-parental conflict, the child should show fewer problems. However, other research shows that conflict may sometimes begin at the time of separation and divorce, and that although some parents manage to make harmonious arrangements for their children, conflict can continue between parents for most of the childhood years.[109] This may lead to the withdrawal of the non-resident parent (usually the father) as an available source of support for the child.[110]

The Amato[111] meta-analysis reports on eight studies that look at outcomes for children in high conflict intact families, low conflict intact families and divorced families. Studies carried out in the UK by Jenkins and Smith,[112] and studies described by Richards,[113] have also found differences in outcomes between children in intact families who experience high or low levels of conflict.

From the studies he has reviewed, Amato summarises that not only did children in high conflict intact families have worse outcomes than children in low conflict intact families, they also showed lower levels of well-being than children in divorced families overall. These studies did not look at children's well-being according to the different groups formed in re-ordered families, such as lone parents, step families and re-disrupted families.

Studies by Camara and Resnick[114] found that family type was also associated with poorer outcomes for children; when family conflict was added to the equation its effect ruled out other factors. Studies by Block et al.[115] on boys living in high conflict intact families looked at the behaviour of these children in intact families before parental separation, and concluded that evidence of behavioural difficulties existed pre-divorce for those children who had most problems after divorce. Hetherington's longitudinal studies[116] discuss the fact that if children are exposed to high conflict before divorce, this should improve for the children after divorce, when the conflict is presumed to subside.

The Amato analysis also looks at studies reporting on continuing conflict between parents after divorce and the effect this has on children (Kurdek and Berg;[117] Luepnitz;[118] Johnson et al.[119]). A study by Guidubaldi et al.[120] showed that boys responded better when parental conflict was lower post-divorce, but that protracted conflict had less effect on girls. In a comparison study by Hess and Camara,[121] the importance of parental co-operation post-divorce was also found to be important, but did not differentiate between boys and girls.

An important finding by Hodges[122] was that where mothers reported conflict with their ex-spouse, this did not correlate with the child's adjustment, i.e. the mother's report of conflict between herself and her ex-partner did not necessarily correspond with the child's view or experience of conflict between the parents. Parental conflict has been singled out in all studies about families and children as one of the most important factors affecting a child's behaviour and adjustment, either within marriage or beyond it. In some studies, exposure to conflict rather than family type has been shown to be the strongest influence on children's adjustment.[123]

Children's responses and outcomes

In their longitudinal studies, Wallerstein and Kelly,[124] Wallerstein et al.[125] and Hetherington[126] looked at the effects of parental separation from the child's view. Studies carried out in New Zealand, particularly the Fergusson study,[8] and in Australia by Dunlop and Burns,[127] also sought the views of the child. In the UK, such studies have been carried out by Mitchell[128] and by Walczak and Burns.[129]

These studies asked children about their experience of life after separation and divorce, their views on their involvement in plans for their future, how the separation was explained to them and their views about contact arrangements. Children were also asked about the kinds of difficulties they experienced generally, as a result of separation and divorce.[130]

Other studies carried out by Rutter et al.,[131] have looked at the complex relationship between stressful life factors and the child's ability to withstand, or be affected by, the kinds of events that happen in their lives. Studies that have paid particular attention to this include those by Jenkins and Smith,[132] Capaldi[133] and Peterson et al.[134] (USA) and the relationship has been discussed widely by Wallerstein et al.,[135] Wallerstein and Kelly[136] and Hetherington et al.,[137] who have attempted to assess some of the factors that contribute to the child's well-being and adaption over time and why some children will continue to have problems, 5 to 10 years after their parents have divorced.

Other studies have highlighted the importance of protective factors, such as a good relationship with one parent or with both parents, or a good and supportive relationship with siblings or other significant adults.[138] In a study carried out by Guidubaldi et al.,[139] lowered self-esteem was linked to more disruptive behaviour at school. These studies have also looked at the importance of reinforcement at school as being most valuable to children who have the lowest self-esteem. Interventions have been shown to be least effective for children who live in low conflict marriages with fewest problems, and most effective for children who experience the most conflict and disruption.

Longitudinal studies such as Hetherington's[140] and a study carried out by Camara,[141] as well as studies in the UK by Wadsworth[142] and Chase-Lansdale et al.,[143] have shown that "academic competence" is definitely reduced following separation and divorce. The actual differences are probably small and variable in different studies, but all studies report that problems at school are not explained by socio-economic variables alone, and family type is not always the key factor.

Since 1930, marital status in the USA has been a more predictive factor than race as to the number of years that children spend at school (i.e. continuing with further or higher education). Longitudinal studies in the UK[144] would also support the theory that the child's chances of further education are reduced by the fact of

parental divorce. Children's performance at school may also be affected by the teacher's reaction to, and expectations of, children living in different family groups; teachers may have lower expectations of children living in separated/divorced families.[145]

Problems with self-esteem have been reported in various studies to be associated with change in marital status and as a response to parental conflict. Other life stresses have also been shown to affect the child's sense of well-being. A study carried out by Raschke et al.[146] showed no difference in problems with self-esteem according to family type but problems with self-esteem were related to the levels of parental conflict, regardless of whether the child lived in a divorced or a two-parent family, and to the child's relationship with its resident parent.[147]

"Over the passage of time parental conflict and remarriage seemed to be [the most] salient predictors of lowered self-image".[148] Longitudinal studies suggest that children who experience divorce or high conflict show more *"depression and withdrawn responses"* (Peterson and Zill).[149]

Wallerstein and Kelly[150] also found depression and withdrawal more common in children who had experienced parental divorce. They point out that parents are unaware of the level of difficulties in their child concerning self-esteem, so the child's data is more reliable.[151] Studies by Kalter and Watt[152] in the USA and Jenkins and Smith[153] in the UK discuss children's externalised and internalised behaviours linked to self-esteem, and suggest ways of enhancing self-esteem through reinforcement at school.

Other studies show that parents and teachers are more likely to respond to "externalised behaviour", such as conduct disorders, hostility and antagonism, rather than the more withdrawn behaviours connected with lowered self-esteem. Problems with self-esteem present a complex picture for researchers: is it that lowered self-esteem leads to feelings of non-well-being, lack of confidence at school, inability to make friends, and psychosomatic health problems, or is it these factors in themselves that cause low self-esteem?

Another important factor addressed by research is the age of the child at the time of separation and divorce. Wallerstein and Kelly[154] suggest clear differences in children's understanding, acceptance and concept of divorce, at different ages, and these are regarded by them as important predictions of later adjustments.[155] They and others recognise important effects of the length of time since separation and of the current age of the child at assessment.

Wallerstein and Kelly,[156] and reviews by both Emery[157] and Hodges,[158] emphasise the importance of children's responses at different ages to separation and divorce. Children as young as two and a half years, will be aware of parental conflict and will respond to their parents' difficulties. Children aged five or six may more often blame themselves, and older children (pre-adolescent) tend to blame one parent and be supportive to the other. Adolescents may be very angry with their parents (Wallerstein and Kelly[159]) but the interaction between the age of the child at time of separation and the passage of time since the divorce is very complex, as reported by Emery[160] in his review of studies. Emery summarised his findings by concluding that there have been relatively few successful attempts to untangle these effects.

In a National cohort study reported by Zill[161] in the USA, 14 per cent of parents in re-ordered families believed their children had experienced emotional problems and needed help in the past year, and 13 per cent had seen a mental health professional. This compared to 6 per cent from intact families. Similar findings have been reported by Wadsworth et al.[162] and by Kalter et al.,[163] which suggest that children of separated families are over-represented in mental health clinics. This is also discussed by Emery[164] in his review. Other studies find that children from re-ordered families, and particularly those who experience the remarriage and/or subsequent re-ordering of their parents' relationships, are more likely to experience Social Service intervention and are over-represented among the young homeless.[165]

Parents particularly report difficulties with behaviour immediately after divorce and, subsequently, before or after contact visits with the non-resident parent. Non-resident parents describe children as being awkward and miserable when it is time for the child to return to their resident parent. Residual behavioural difficulties are reported by parents in both the Wallerstein and Kelly[166] and Hetherington et al.[167] studies. But Emery's[168] review of the literature emphasises the difficulties that parents, teachers and professionals have in deciding, especially with adolescents, what is normal behaviour and what is an abnormal or particular response to the life stresses the child is experiencing.[169] Perhaps more than in any other response of the child to the experience of conflict and family re-organisation, the inter-relationships make it difficult to assess the "correlation and causal factors" affecting the child's behaviour.

Remarriage

"The presence of children may pre-dispose a second marriage to failure."[170]

Although there has been considerable research into the break-down of marriage, there has been less on the effects of remarriage on children. Robinson and Smith[171] report that there is doubt and confusion about the roles of step-parents and the roles they should play in relation to step-children who become part of the new family group, either resident or visiting. Research by Visher and Visher,[172] Furstenberg[173] and Burgoyne and Clark[174] highlight particular problems for step-parents.

These studies find that there are more problems in what are described as "complex" step-families, where both partners have children, who spend all or some of their time in the new family. There are more problems for boys in relation to step-fathers in terms of discipline and authority and maintaining their own relationship with the non-resident parent. There are problems in terms of the very nature of a step-family in comparison to intact families.[175]

Some studies have said that there should be no comparison between an intact two-parent family and a two-parent remarried family, as the differences between them are so great. However, according to Furstenberg et al.[176] *"Remarried couples face the same dilemmas as in their first marriage, i.e. trying to develop a shared and joint view of the world but they just come to this shared view by a different route."*

In their research into step-families, Visher and Visher[177] discuss the effects of children on the couple and the difficulties of working out the relationships between the parents, step- and half-siblings and resident or visiting children. Furstenberg et al.[178] describes the much more complex views held by each parent, and associates a higher breakdown of second marriages to the fact that parents who remarry are those who have been more willing to leave a first unhappy marriage. They are therefore more willing to face a second break-down rather than stay in an unfulfilling relationship.

Other studies[179] have looked at the different ages of children in response to the marriage of their parents. Younger children seem to have less difficulty in adapting, even when they have a good relationship with the non-resident parent. Teenagers have much more difficulty in adapting to the remarriage of either parent. Parent dating, which precedes repartnering or remarriage,

The Exeter Family Study

presents difficulties for adolescents and overt displays of affection between a new parent and a potential new partner can impinge on the adolescent's emerging sexual development. The very presence of a romantic interest obliges the child to face the fact that reconciliation between its parents is impossible.[180] Boys appear to form better relationships with a step-father, even though they have a good relationship with their own non-resident parent, than girls who obtain a new step-mother.

Legal research

Previous research has also looked at the links between the kinds of decisions that are made at the time of separation and divorce (Davis and Murch in the UK and Pearson in the USA[181]).

Development and changes in the justice system and legal profession in the way in which the dissolution of marriage and family structures is approached, have been well documented in the literature associated with the construction and implementation of the Children Act (1989).[182] Divorce law and the emergence of differing approaches to conflict resolution, and the need to encourage families to co-operate rather than adopt the adversarial approach, is also looked at in studies by Davis and Murch.[183] The changing and developing nature of both private and public law relating to families and children is discussed fully and updated in *The Family Justice System* by Murch and Hooper.[184]

The emergence of mediation services, with the emphasis on the need to keep the child at the centre of negotiation, has been recorded by Parkinson,[185] Fisher[186] and Roberts.[187] Evaluation of the effectiveness of new and developing approaches to mediation has been undertaken by Roberts[188] and Davis[189] in the UK and by Pearson in the USA.[190]

Research into the effects of mediation, and its cost, has been carried out by Walker et al.,[191] who also looked at different models of mediation. Research in the USA has shown that the quality of the service given to couples –whether the decision was mediated or adjudicated – is reflected in the outcomes.[192] This group (as well as Kelly) has also researched the quality of In-court Mediation, the importance of welfare reports and whether these provide an effective knowledge base upon which the judge may make decisions.[193]

1 Schaffer, H.R. (1990). A review and disussion about making decisions for children after divorce.

2 Furstenberg Jnr., F.F. & Cherlin, A.J. (1991).

3 Kalter, N. et al. (1989).

4 Hetherington, E.M. et al. (1985); Wallerstein, J.S. & Kelly, J.B. (1980); Guidubaldi, J. et al. (1987); Wallerstein, J.S. et al. (1986); Zill, N. (1988).

5 Ferri, E. et al. (1993).

6 Wadsworth, M.E.J. (1991). An assessment of both short and long term effects on children after divorce.

7 Kiernan, K.E. et al. (1991).

8 Fergusson, D.M. & Dimond, M.E. (1986). A cohort study based on 1,200 New Zealand children born in 1980.

9 Furstenberg, F.F. & Allison, P.D. (1985).

10 Kalter, N. (1987).

11 McLanahan, S.S. (1985). See also McLanahan, S.S. & Bumpass, L. (1988); Amato, P. & Bruce, K. (1991).

12 Douglas, J.W.B. (1970, 1973) health outcome for the children who had experienced divorce before the age of six (e.g. higher risk of bed wetting, etc.).

13 Wadsworth, M.E.J. (1986). An overview of the findings of the 1946 cohort studies. See also Amato, P. & Bruce, K. (1991). An analysis of studies which have assessed the effects of family reorganisation on children, and the consequences in economic and psychological terms.

14 Hetherington, E.M. et al. (1985). A paper which presents some of the long-term negative outcomes for children following divorce.

15 Chester, R. (1979). The effects of separation and divorce on parental health and use of medical services.

16 Wadsworth, M.E.J. et al. (1986).

17 Dominian, J. et al. (1991). A response to the Department of Health document, *Health of the Nation*, emphasising the social, emotional and health costs of family breakdown for men, women and children.

18 Furstenberg, F.F. (1979, 1982, 1988).

19 Wadsworth, M.E.J. et al. (1991).

20 Kuh, D. & MacLean, M. (1990).

21 Kiernan, K.E. et al. (1991).

22 Ferri, E. (1993). See also Butler, N. (1986).

23 Wallerstein, J.S. & Kelly, J.B. (1980).

24 Kalter, N. (1987).

25 Rutter, M. (1989) The importance of protective factors and the child's vulnerability are discussed in relation to adverse life events.

26 Goodyer (1990). A paper looking at the complexity of the association of life events on children's outcomes and their vulnerability and adaptive mechanisms.

27 Guidubaldi, J. et al. (1987).

28 Capaldi, D.M. (1989).

29 See Kalter, N. et al. (1989).

30 Emery, R. E. (1988). A review of studies which have looked at the complex issues surrounding family breakdown and reorganisation.

31 Amato, P. & Bruce, K. (1991).

32 Amato, P. & Bruce, K. (1991).

33 Emery, R. E. (1988).

34 Pasley, K. & Ihinger-Tallman, M. (1987). Discussion about the complexities of remarriage and step-parenting illustrated by reference to the main studies carried out in the USA and elsewhere.

35 Pasley, K. & Ihinger-Tallman, M. (1987).

36 Ferri, E. (1984). Children living in step-families are reviewed in a national sample and some of the main difficulties highlighted.

37 Bumpass, L. et al. (1984).

38 Peterson, J. et al. (1991).

39 Capaldi, D.M. et al. (1991).

40 Furstenberg, F.F. et al. (1983) This study on remarriage found that 37 per cent of children living in a step-family would experience its breakdown and 10 per cent would experience multiple breakdown. This present study shows a higher number of the study children experiencing multiple disruption.

41 Ferri, E. (1984); Hetherington, E.M. et al. (1992); Bradshaw, J. et al. (1991); Burgoyne, J. & Clark, D. (1984).

42 Capaldi, D.M. et al. (1991); Block, J.H. et al. (1986).

43 Capaldi, D.M. et al. (1991).

44 Hodges, W.F. (1986).

45 Emery, R. E. (1988).

46 Capaldi, D.M. et al. (1991).

47 Furstenberg, F.F. & Nord, C.W. (1985).

48 Walzack, Y. & Burns, S. (1984). A qualitative account of 100 children's views of their parents divorce.

49 Burgoyne, J. & Clark, D. (1984); Burgoyne, J. et al. (1987). A British study about the problems facing step-families.

50 Wallerstein, J.S. & Kelly, J.B. (1980). This study also emphasises the lack of preparation and explanation experienced by children after divorce.

51 Furstenberg, F.F. et al. (1987). See also Amato, P. (1993).

52 Amato, P. (1987).

53 Dunlop, R. & Burns, A. (1988).

54 Mitchell, A. (1985). A similar study carried out in Scotland, which showed that children felt excluded from parental management of divorce and, like the children in the present study, would have liked more contact with their non-resident parent.

55 Wallerstein, J.S. & Kelly, J.B. (1980).

56 Hetherington, E.M. et al. (1985).

57 Wadsworth, M.E.J. et al. (1986). A presentation of the long-term effects of parental divorce on children's life chances.

58 Schaffer, H.R. (1990).

59 Richards, M. (1987). Examines the importance of the child's biological parents and the changing structure of "family" and how divorce alters perceptions of parenthood.

60 Bowlby, J. (1982). A later review of the attachment and loss theories also discussed in Karen, R. (1994).

61 Richards, M. (1987).

62 Schaffer, H.R. (1990).

63 Hetherington, E.M. et al. (1985); Wallerstein, J.S. & Kelly, J.B. (1980).

64 Hetherington, E.M. et al. (1992). Looks at the effects on children of separation, divorce, lone parenthood and remarriage are looked at longitudinally with particular emphasis on a child's behaviour response and on the age of the children at separation.

65 Wadsworth, M.E.J. et al. (1986).

66 Wallerstein, J.S. & Kelly, J.B. (1980).

67 Capaldi, D.M. (1989); Peterson, J. & Zill, N. (1991). These studies looked at the differing responses of boys and girls living with the different/same sex parent and who may have experienced multiple re-ordering.

68 Wallerstein, J.S. & Kelly, J.B. (1980).

69 Hetherington, E.M. et al. (1992).

70 Pasley, K. et al. (1987).

71 Furstenberg, F.F. & Nord C.W (1985). The importance of contact with both parents post-divorce and the difficulties of post-divorce parenting are described in this study and the non-resident parents interviewed in the present study described similar difficulties.

72 Hodges, W.F. (1986).

73 Wallerstein, J.S. & Kelly, J.B. (1980).

74 Hetherington, E.M. (1992).

75 Richards, M. (1987).

76 Furstenberg, F.F. & Spanier, S.B. (1984). This paper reports on the problems of step-parenting and the child's relationship with the non-resident parents; and the effects this has on the child's resident parents relationship (with the child).

77 Willmott, P. (1986) This study examines the frequency of support and initiatives offered between close relatives. See also Finch, J. et al. (1993), which discusses and reinforces the importance of intergenerational links and maintaining them through family transitions (not only divorce). The present study emphasises the importance of local family contacts and the difficulty of keeping in touch with non-resident parent/grandparents after divorce.

78 Cherlin, A.J. & Furstenberg, F. (1986). This paper, entitled The New American Grandparent, puts forward the view that little is done to encourage continued contact after divorce with non-resident parents/relatives and that children may lose touch with a succession of important and supportive kinship networks. See also Furstenberg, F.F. & Spanier, S.B. (1984).

79 Cherlin, A.J. et al. (1986).

80 Bradshaw, J. et al. (1991). Concentrating on the effects of poverty on family life this study emphasises the link between lone parenthood, low maintenance payments and deprivation.

81 Jacobs, J.A. & Furstenberg, F.F. Jnr. (1986).

82 Kalter, N. et al. (1987, 1989).

83 Wallerstein, J.S. & Kelly, J.B. (1980); Hetherington, E.M. et al. (1982).

84 Bradshaw, J. & Millar, J. (1991).

85 Hetherington, E.M. (1992); Wadsworth, M.E.J. (1991).

86 Amato, P. & Bruce, K. (1991).

87 Hodges, W.F. (1986).

88 Emery, R. E. (1988).

89 Dunlop, R. & Burns, A. (1983).

90 Hodges, W.F. (1978).

91 Amato, P. & Bruce, K. (1991).

92 Guidubaldi, J. et al. (1983, 1987).

93 Dunlop, R. & Burns, A. (1983).

94 Peterson, J. & Zill, N. (1986).

95 Camara, K.A. & Resnick, G. (1988).

96 Santrock, J.W. & Warshak, R. (1979); Warshak, R. & Santrock, J.W. (1983) re: the effects of mother-custody and father-custody homes on children's outcomes.

97 Hetherington, E.M. (1986).

98 Wallerstein, J.S. & Kelly, J.B. (1980).

99 Emery, R.E. (1988).

100 Jenkins, M. & Smith, M.A. (1991). High conflict in intact families associated with poorer behavioural and school outcomes reported in this paper is also found in the present study.

101 Dunlop, R. & Burns, A. (1983, 1988).

102 Kiernan, K.E. & Chase-Lansdale, P. (1991).

103 Cherlin, A. et al. (1991); Amato, P. & Bruce, K. (1991); Camara, K.A. & Resnick, G. (1988); Block, J.H. et al. (1986).

104 Kurdek, L.A., Blisk, D. & Seisky, A.E. (1981) This study found that conflict present before the divorce may be reduced by divorce for some children but for others it was an indicator of future difficulties.

105 Parish, T. & and Wigle, S. (1985). A further investigation of the important mediating effect of self-esteem on other outcomes for children.

106 Hetherington, E.M. et al. (1992).

107 Wadsworth, M.E.J. (1991).

108 Kelly, J.B. (1982).

109 Ahrons, S.C.R. & Rodgers, R. (1987); Schaffer, H.R. (1990).

110 Kalter, N. (1987).

111 Amato, P. & Bruce, K. (1991).

112 Jenkins, J.M. & Smith, M.A. (1991).

The Exeter Family Study

113   Richards, M. (1987).

114   Camara, K.A. & Resnick, G. (1988). Family conflict whether in intact or re-ordered families was found in this study to outweigh other negative factors; gender issues re: same-sex parent were also examined.

115   Block, J.H. et al. (1986). Problems were found to exist pre-divorce for children in this study of boys, post-divorce, with continuing problems.

116   Hetherington, E.M.'s longitudinal studies, as presented in the monograph Coping with Marital Transitions (Hetherington, E.M. et al. (1992)).

117   Kurdek, L.A. & Berg, B. (1983). The effects of continuing conflict post-divorce, and its effects on outcomes showed that a poor relationship with the non-resident parent had little effect.

118   Luepnitz, D.A. (1982). Also found little association between good contact and outcome for children. The present study found that children had fewer problems when parents communicated about contact.

119   Johnson, A.J.R. et al. (1985). This study found that increased contact was associated with problems for the child.

120   Guidubaldi, J. et al. (1987).

121   Hess, R.D. & Camara, K.A. (1979).

122   Hodges, W.F. (1983).

123   Amato, P. & Bruce, K. (1991); Hodges, W.F. (1987).

124   Wallerstein, J.S. & Kelly, J.B. (1980). Qualitative data on the child's difficulties adapting to parental change.

125   Wallerstein, J.S. et al. (1989). A qualitative account records parents and childrens adaption to divorce over time.

126   Hetherington, E.M. et al. (1985).

127   Dunlop, R. & Burns, A. (1988). This Australian study shows little difference between children in intact and re-ordered families on some measures. These findings are partly supported by the present study.

128   Mitchell, A. (1985). A qualitative British account of the child's view of parental separation supports many of the findings of the present study.

129   Walczak, Y. & Burns, S. (1984). See also Mitchell, A. (1985); Burgoyne, J. et al. (1987) for discussion about the child's response to divorce.

130   Emery, R.E. (1988).

131   Rutter, M. et al. (1985) explores the link between the child's personality and resistance to adverse life events. See also Goodyer, I. (1990) re: the complex links between life events and children's outcomes in a study of a clinical sample.

132   Jenkins, J.M. & Smith, M.A. (1991).

133   Capaldi, D.M. (1991). The complex nature of the differing responses to children in adverse circumstances is examined; also the importance of protective factors.

134   Peterson, J. et al. (1986).

135   Wallerstein, J.S. et al. (1989).

136   Wallerstein, J.S. & Kelly, J.B. (1980).

137   Hetherington, E.M. et al. (1992).

138   Jenkins, J.M. & Smith, M.A. (1991); Rutter, M. (1981); Watt, N. et al. (1989). School as an arena for reinforcement for vulnerable children is highlighted by these three studies.

139   Guidubaldi, J. et al. (1984).

140   Hetherington, E.M. (1986).

141   Camara, K.A. (1981). Educational failure and family status especially at the acute stage of family breakdown are shown to be associated in this study, as in other British and American longitudinal studies.

142   Wadsworth, M.E.J. (1987).

143   Kiernan, K.E. & Chase-Lansdale (1991).

144   Wadsworth, M.E.J. et al. (1987); Ferri, E. (1993); Chase-Lansdale, P.L. & Hetherington, E.M. (1990).

145   Touliatos, J. et al. (1980). This study found that teachers' knowledge of the child's family status affected teachers' expectations and response to the child. This was not evident in the present study.

146   Raschke, H.J. & Raschke, V.J. (1979). Self-image as an indicator of the vulnerability to parental conflict is seen as a negative factor in this study.

147   Parish, T. et al. (1980).

148   Parish, T. & Dostal, J. (1980). This study assesses the link between self-esteem and the quality of the child's relationship with both parents, either in an intact family or after divorce.

149   Peterson, J. & Zill, N. (1986).

150   Wallerstein, J.S. & Kelly, J.B. (1980).

151   Emery, R.E. (1988); Rutter, M. (1985, 1989).

152   Kalter, N. (1987); Watt, N. et al. (1989).

153   Jenkins, J.M. & Smith, M.A. (1991).

154   Wallerstein, J.S. & Kelly, J.B. (1980).

155   Hetherington, E.M. et al. (1992).

156   Wallerstein, J.S. & Kelly, J.B. (1980).

157   Emery, R. E. (1988).

158   Hodges, W.F. (1986).

159   Wallerstein, J.S. & Kelly, J.B. (1980).

160   Emery, R. E. (1988).

161   Zill, N. (1978). This study shows that children post-divorce are more vulnerable to psychiatric interventions..

162   Wadsworth, M.E.J. et al. (1986).

163   Kalter, N. et al. (1981). An American study looking at the increased risk of psychiatric disturbance of children in re-ordered families based on a psychiatric outpatient clinic sample.

164   Emery, R.E. (1988).

165   Bebbington, A. & Miles, J. et al. (1988). Shows an over-representation of children from step-families and re-disrupted families among the young homeless.

166   Wallerstein, J.S. & Kelly, J.B. (1980).

167   Hetherington, E.M. et al. (1992).

168   Emery, R. E. (1988).

169   Rutter, M. (1976). Discusses adolescence as a normal transition or a behavioural response to parental and/or societal pressures and looks at aspects of adolescent adaption.

170   Emery, R.E. (1988).

171   Robinson, M. & Smith, D. (1993). The authors are experienced family therapists working closely with step-families to support parents and children. The difficulties facing step-families are fully explored along with some positive benefits to the children.

172   Visher, E.B. & Visher, J.S. (1979, 1985). American studies with a practitioners' view of step-parenting. Step-parents in the present study did express concerns about the lack of available help to help clarify issues between step-parents and the children.

173   Furstenberg, F.F. (1981). Looks at the complexities of re-ordering, the expectation of parents of a second marriage, the likelihood of break-down and the importance of the interaction of children within step-families.

174   Burgoyne, J. & Clark, D. (1984).

175   Santrock, J.W. & Sitterle, K. (1987). Step-families in the present study reported some changed attitudes to the second marriage but were still less satisfied with sharing of tasks than intact families.

175   Furstenberg, F.F. et al. (1982).

177   Visher, E.B. & Visher, J.S. (1979, 1985); Chilman et al. (1988), where the issues of treating the more serious maladaptions to step-family life are discussed.

178   Furstenberg, F.F. et al. (1982).

179   Hetherington, E.M. (1987); Ahrons, S.C.R. & Rodgers, R. et al. (1987) reviewed in Pasley, K. et al. (1987).

180　Kalter, N. (1993).

181　Davis, G. & Murch, M. (1988); Pearson, J. (1982, 1989, 1991) in the USA.

182　Davis, G. & Roberts, M. (1989).

183　Davis, G. & Murch, M. (1988).

184　Murch, M. & Hooper, (1988). Consultation with the judiciary, family lawyers, mediators and researchers provides an imaginative and directional over-view of the complexities of family law "in a state of flux".

185　Parkinson, L. (1989).

186　Fisher, T. (1992).

187　Roberts, M. (1988).

188　Roberts, M. (1988).

189　Davis, G. & Roberts, M. (1989).

190　Pearson, J. (1988). An evaluation of mediated divorce settlements.

191　Walker, et al. (1989/1994) Comprehensive mediation established with the legal profession by the FMA was piloted by the NFM service and evaluated by Walker et al. where families found mediation a better alternative particularly concerning child-related issues.

192　Pearson, J. (1993). The reasons that parents return to court for an adjustment to an original order are explored and clarified with some surprising results, e.g. defined access orders work better for some parents than undefined ones.

193　Kelly, J.B. (1991). A comparison of outcomes following mediated or adversarial divorce resolution for families.

Methods

The study took place during 1990–2; the interviews were held in 1991. The Local Education Authority was aware of, and supported, the study and approval was also received from the Exeter Research Ethics Committee. The study was supported by national and local advisory groups, who were involved in discussions about methodology and progress. The national advisory group included representatives from research educational practice, mediation services and other family support systems. The local advisory group included a head teacher, a psychologist, an adviser for educational special needs and a family doctor.

The study population

Following discussions with both advisory groups, it was decided to approach schools in a specific geographical area to ask for their help. The sample includes two age groups (9–10 years and 13–14 years; school years 5 and 9), so that both high schools and their feeder middle schools were included.

Exeter operates a four-tier education system:

1. Primary school: 5 to 8 years ⎫ may be on the
2 Middle school: 8 to 12 years ⎬ same site or
                                ⎭ combined

3 High school: 12 to 16 years

4 Sixth Form College: 16+

In this pilot study it was decided to interview two separate age groups of children (the age groups being chosen in relation to school milestones); the groups we studied were 9 to 10 year olds at the top end of the middle school system where problems can start to become entrenched, and 13 to 14 year olds in the second year of high school, where problems can either dissipate or become more overt. The latter age group is also a time when problems with friendships and self-esteem become more evident.

Short questionnaires were sent to all the parents of children in the two year groups. Information sent out with the questionnaire assured parents that the questionnaires were confidential and that any information would not be shared with school. It was also explained to the parents, that the research team might later approach them for further help, but that the decision to help could be made by the family at a later date. Information about the department and details of previous research were also included. The questionnaire asked parents about the child's family, health, school, social activities, occupation of parents, income and living circumstances.

The participants

Almost 1,000 questionnaires were sent out by the 13 schools and 750 were returned, of which 621 had been completed, 429 questionnaires were returned from intact families and 188 from re-ordered families. These numbers do not necessarily accurately reflect prevalence of each family type, but do appear to be fairly representative, based on our knowledge of demographic data (National Household Survey/ Census).

Two independent schools returned a much higher rate of intact family questionnaires (44 and 29 from intact families as opposed to 13 and 6 from re-ordered families). This may reflect a different proportion of re-ordered families or a greater reluctance by such parents in independent schools to participate. Descriptive data about the children and families who responded to the initial questionnaire are shown in Table 1.

Census information from the Exeter District for the age group 10–14 years showed that there were 2,705 boys and 2,576 girls; no information was available to enable the numbers to be divided into the exact groups looked at in the study.

The study groups

The aim of the study was to compare and contrast family experiences and difficulties according to the family groups that children lived in. A matched pair protocol was adopted to minimise the effect of several potentially important variables.

Table 1 Children in families completing first questionnaire

		INTACT		RE-ORDERED		EXETER DISTRICT
		Total	Matched	Total	Matched	
Number in each family type		429	76	188	76	**25595
Sex:						
	Boys	197	36	77	36	
	Girls	232	40	111	40	
Age group						
	9–10 years	157	34	74	34	
	13–14 years	272	42	114	42	
Mother's education						
	left school at 16	246	56	131	61	
	higher education or vocational	59	7	15	6	
	tertiary	120	11	33	8	
	not known	4	2	9	1	
Position in family:						
	Only child	17	3	20	4	
	Eldest child	157	28	71	27	
	Other	253	45	95	45	
	Not known	2		2		
School:						
	State	299	71	153	70	
	Independent	130	5	35	6	
Social Class:						
	Group I (1, 2, 3)	262	31	73	26	21639
	Group II (3m, 4, 5)	135	38	68	35	17828
	Group III (Other)	21	6	32	14	924
	Not known	11	1	5	1	
*Accommodation:						
	Owner occupier	355	57	112	44	27714
	Private tenant	14	1	10	4	4193
	Council tenant	53	15	59	25	8378
	Other	7	3	7	3	491
*Net Income:						
	Less £90	11	3	41	16	
	£90–£135	33	13	35	17	
	Up to £150	65	20	15	11	
	£160 plus	301	37	75	26	
	Not known	19	3	12	6	

*Not used in matching

**The numbers for the Exeter District are based on 1991 census figures (study carried out 1990–2). Numbers show that, in the Exeter district, 22,068 parents were living in "married" households, and 3,527 parents were living in "divorced" households.

Pairs were selected by matching on all of the criteria in the following list derived from groupings, as appropriate, of variables in Table 1 with one of each pair living in a re-ordered family and one in an intact family. Only families where parents were living together at the time of the child's birth were included.

Matching criteria:

Sex	(boy/girl)
Age	(9+ years.13+ years)
Mother's education	(left school<16 years, higher education)
Position in family	(eldest or single/other)
School	(state, independent)
Social Class group	(as in Table 1: A, B, C)

The sample was stratified to include roughly equal numbers of pairs where one had experienced separation or divorce before or after the age of five, and for the social class groupings non-manual and manual.

The level of mother's education was given a high priority in the matching process as this is believed to be the best of the socio-demographic variables available to us from the first questionnaire in predicting quality of child care. It was also a factor unaffected by family breakdown and remains a significant influence in the child's life. (Six children in the study lived with their fathers, three of whom had frequent contact with their mother.)

In contrast, the social class of current head of household was broadly grouped into only two main categories. As downward social mobility is more likely to occur in families where the couple has divorced, the effects of divorce on the well-being of their children will, if anything, be under-estimated. In total, 184 families were identified and contacted, and of these 174 agreed to be interviewed. Twenty-two were not included in the analysis for various reasons associated with incorrect matching on review of the data with the family.

It had already been suggested that such a study about separation and divorce would be difficult because the subject was likely to cause pain for both parents and children. When parents were approached about the study they had received written information about the previous work of the department (sent with the initial questionnaire) and about the emphasis placed by the department on action research. The refusal rate was very low; of the 184 families approached only two refused because the they felt study was intrusive. The other eight families who declined decided not to take part because of major events that were happening to them at the time. These included grandparents' illness, house renovations, a child being statemented and undergoing tests, and the illness of a parent. One family declined because: "*The house is falling down and has to be propped up*". The research team hoped that the family had not been driven to exaggeration to escape participation, but their explanation, in fact, was absolutely true!

It was decided by the research team that the resident parent would be asked to contact the natural father/mother to seek permission for interview, rather than making a direct approach. Relationships between parents, and contact arrangements, were sometimes fragile and we did not wish the research to exacerbate any difficulties.

If the non-resident parent agreed to take part in the study, all the information that had been sent to the resident parent at the initial stage was forwarded to the non-resident parent, followed by a visit to confirm interview arrangements. Twenty-seven out of a possible 41 non-resident parents willing to be interviewed are included in the study; all but three live locally. The same questionnaire was used for both parents, so that information collected formally precisely coincided. Twenty-six non-resident parents were "matched" with the child's resident parent. One resident parent was not included in the comparison data because the child was not included in the matched pair group.

Interviews

Parents of children selected for inclusion in the main study by the matching process were visited and asked if they would be willing to take part in the second stage of the study. The purpose of the study was explained and any queries were answered.

Three hundred and seventy in-depth interviews were carried out, lasting, on average, 2 hours for the parents and 1 hour for the child; some parental interviews were much longer – 4 hours or more. The number of interviews completed were as follows:

- 174 family interviews.

- 170 child interviews.

- 27 non-resident parent interviews.

There were some difficulties in interviewing the non-resident parent group (Table 2) but there were no refusals from the non-resident parents once contact had been established.

Table 2 **Non-resident parents**		
1	Interviews completed	27
2	Mother refused permission to contact father	11
3	Father deceased – after divorce	2
4	No contact with non-resident parent	17
5	Out of area	5
6	Not found after several visits	14
	Total	**76**

After each interview, an individual letter was sent to each parent and child thanking them for their help; both parents and children were invited to contact the department if they had any queries or worries about the interviews.

Interviews took place by appointment at the families' homes. Parents were asked if they would discuss with their child whether the child would agree to be included in the study. Parents were always interviewed first and, if the parent and their child were willing, a further appointment was made for the child to be interviewed. Almost all the 13- to 14-year-olds were interviewed alone. Parents of the younger age group (9 to 10 years) sometimes, though not always, remained in the room for the beginning of the interview, but left the interviewer alone with the child if the child seemed comfortable. A small proportion of parents remained for the whole of the interview. Sometimes brothers and sisters came in, but never stayed for the whole of the interview, so that sensitive questions were postponed until an appropriate time.

Although many parents were initially wary, interviews were universally well received and apparently appreciated by interviewees, many expressing their thanks formally for having been listened to; this was particularly true of the non-resident parent, most of whom felt they had never been asked their views about their child. Non-resident parent interviews were long, lasting 2 to 3 hours, and in a quarter of cases, were carried out in the presence of new partners. In one instance, where contact was limited to once a year, the interview was inevitably brief because of lack of knowledge. *"Every other parent you talk to will know more than me"* was the non-resident parent's comment.

School and medical questionnaires

In order to obtain an independent view of the child's progress, and to follow on from the initial work with schools to recruit the study group, schools were approached, with parental permission, to ask the child's form teacher to complete a questionnaire about the child's progress. Teachers worked with the research team to design a questionnaire to be sent to schools.

The child's family doctor was also asked to complete a short questionnaire about the child's health. A family doctor worked with the research team to compile the questionnaire.

These parts of the study were carried out under the same strict rules of confidentiality.

All head teachers were co-operative and supported the study; in some instances tutors and year heads felt unable to complete the questionnaires, mainly through pressure of work in establishing the National Curriculum, and in some cases where they felt that they did not wish to complete such a personal questionnaire.

Both parents and teachers were reassured about the confidential nature of the study. In one case the school staff decided to return none of the questionnaires. One high school returned only a quarter; there was a higher rate of return from other schools.

Most doctors were very co-operative in spite of the time involved in completing the questionnaire and we gratefully acknowledge their co-operation. Pressure of work rather than any ideological reasons accounted for the incomplete return of the questionnaires.

The parents

The parents were co-operative, honest and open with the research team. Research involving face-to-face interviews is time-consuming, but parents were willing to give up time during the day, or more usually evenings, to talk to the research worker. They were willing to talk about their children, the events that had affected family life and to describe the effects on their children. Those who had experienced separation and divorce talked about the difficulties they had encountered, their feelings about the disruption to their lives and their efforts to start again.

The children

Most importantly, nearly all parents were willing to ask their children if they would take part in the research. No interview was carried out if the child was in any way hesitant about their own participation. The questionnaire was discussed with parents, and parents were given the choice of remaining with the child during the interview if there were any concerns.

In many instances children from the same school talked to each other about the interviews and were pleased to say they were included: *"I told my friend that you were coming to see me – you saw her last week"*. There was no feeling that the children had found the interviews difficult. There were some areas in the questionnaire that some children did not want to talk about and their wishes were always respected.

The older age group were actively pleased to be asked about their views and felt that it was an opportunity not often afforded them. Children were assured of the confidential nature of the interview. There would be no reporting back to parents or schools. It was an opportunity for them to say what they felt.

In one family, where both parents had been interviewed plus the study child, the other child of the family felt left out and would have liked to have been included.

Family composition

There were 76 children who had lived with both natural parents since birth and 76 children who had experienced family change (see Table 2.1). Thirty children lived with their mother and new partner, and 39 children lived alone with their mothers in a single parent household. In some cases, mothers had new relationships but these were not "live-in" partners, although they spent some time in the home; the child was able to make a clear distinction between a new parental figure and mother's partner. Mothers did not allow these relationships to become permanent for several reasons: the child sometimes strongly resented their mother's new relationship, or did not like him; other mothers made a conscious decision to remain single and independent. Three mothers had deferred new long-term relationships until their children were older and visited their friends away from the house. Five mothers had never been married to the child's natural father, though had cohabited at least until after the child's birth.

Six children lived with their fathers – three of whom had new partners. One child lived with his father and paternal grandparents. Three maternal grandparents lived with the child and the family – two in re-ordered families and one in an intact family.

One child lived with neither parent because, after the break-up of his mother's second marriage, neither natural parent had wanted the child to live with them. The child now lives with his step-parent and new partner.

Conflict

An important aspect of the study was to look at the effects of parental conflict on children's outcomes; intact families were divided into two groups according to the level of conflict reported by parents (low or high). Children in re-ordered families had experienced conflict which led to the departure of one parent from the home and were therefore divided according to the number of parental transitions.

Analysis of data

The research team looked at the data in two main ways:

1 Whether the child was:

   – normally resident in a family that had been re-ordered because of the departure of one parent since the child's birth (re-ordered family);

   – normally resident with both natural parents (intact family).

2 Subdivision of these two main groups:

   – re-ordered families:

   (i) single parent families where the child lived with a now single parent;

   (ii) step-parent families where the child's resident parent had a new partner (either married or cohabiting);

   (iii) re-disrupted where the child's resident parent's new partnership(s) had broken down;

   – intact families:

   (i) where parents reported no serious rows and no marital problems;

   (ii) where parents reported rows and/or marital problems.

Table 3

| Index child with problem | Control child with problem | |
	Yes	No
No	A	B
Yes	C	D

It was also possible to group the re-ordered families into two main groups:

1 Those who lived with two parents/partners.

2 Those living with one parent.

The former division is used for the main analysis because it allows for the effects of multiple disruption on the child.

In order to take full advantage of the matched pair sample, a McNemar Test was carried out which enabled each child's outcome to be compared directly to its matched pair. Four results were possible:

A Where the control child had a problem and the index child did not.

B Where neither index or control child had a problem.

C Where both the index and control child had a problem.

D Where the index child had a problem and the control child did not.

An odds ratio calculation was then possible between the matched pairs for result D÷A; the numbers of children where both index and control children had problems and the numbers when neither had problems are not included in the equation. In some situations both the index (re-ordered family) and the control (intact family) child have almost similar outcomes; in other instances the odds ratio for a re-ordered family child is several times that for the matched pair intact family child.

Data is examined in this way from the child's point of view, from the parents' point of view and, where available, using the data collected from the family doctor or the school. The data collected from the family doctor and the school was incomplete, which reduced the number of matched pairs for this analysis. Where non-resident parents were also interviewed their responses are matched to those of the resident parent and a McNemar test is again possible ($n = 26$ pairs).

Table 4 Variables entered into multivariate analysis as possible explanatory variables

Variable	Possible values
Child's sex	Male/female
Child's age	9–10/13–14 yrs
Child's position in family	Eldest or only/other
Family type	Re-ordered /intact
Re-ordered sub-type	Intact/single/step/ re-disrupted
Conflict level	High/low
Domestic violence	Yes/no
Mother's education	<16/>16 yrs
1st occupation group	Non-manual/manual/ unemployed
2nd occupation group	Non-manual/other
Gross family income	Four bands
1st financial hardship score	Four bands
2nd financial hardship score	Three bands
Rosenberg self-esteem score	Continuous

Multivariate analysis

In setting up the study it had been expected that a number of different variables describing the child in their family might affect outcomes as explanatory variables. A number of these variables were included in the matching process to reduce the number of confounding variables in interpretation of the results. These are, therefore, controlled for in comparisons of re-ordered and intact families, either in the main or sub-groups. They include:

• The child's age and sex.

• The mother's education (leaving school at 16 or going on to further education).

• The child's position in the family (eldest, only or other)

• The type of school attended (state or independent).

• The occupation of the head of the household (non-manual or other).

Because of matching, none of these factors influence outcomes between comparison groups, but they might be expected to affect outcomes in the group as a whole or within the groups of intact or re-ordered families. It was also expected that other variables would have effects on outcomes that could not be controlled for in the setting up of the comparison (intact) family group. The most important of these is the family structure itself, but others include the level of conflict, the presence of domestic violence in the family and experience of financial hardship.

Self-esteem scores from the child's response to the Rosenberg inventory of questions was intended to be used as an outcome but, as high scores (indicating low self-esteem) on this test were so closely associated with adverse outcomes, this score was also included among the explanatory variables (Table 4).

Linear regressions were carried out using both forward and backward step methods, neither of which make any advance presumptions about the relative importance of different explanatory variables. The outcome variables used were first, scores derived from the adverse outcomes in five areas of the child's life: health (three measures), school (five measures), social (three measures) and behaviour and mood (one measure each). The scores for parent and child data were examined both separately and combined. Secondly, the total number of areas in which an adverse outcome was recorded was also analysed for child, parent and combined data; this prevents undue weighting arising because different areas have different numbers of items scored.

In the child data, the self-esteem score has the closest association with both outcome scores and areas affected, with low self-esteem being significantly related to adverse outcome, whether as total score, or number of areas of the child's life affected. The next most significant explanatory variable is the family structure, with each of the re-ordered family types having a significantly adverse and different magnitude of effect. The largest effect is produced by re-disruption, with living in a single parent or step- family having smaller effect, and being part of a single parent family having a slightly larger effect than living in a step family. The level of the mother's education also has an effect. None of the other possible explanatory variables entered had any significant effects. Violence in the family appears to have a large effect on the outcomes, but after allowing for family type this effect becomes very small in these data.

For parent data, being part of a re-ordered family had the greatest effect, followed by the child's self-esteem score and being in the lower social class group (2nd grouping). For the combined data, self-esteem scores and the type of re-ordered family have the greatest effect on outcomes, as for the child's data, but the social class group also had an effect.

Examining the data in intact families alone, we find that self-esteem has a significant effect in the child's data, while in the parent data only the social class group and child's sex had effects. Although children in high conflict families had some outcomes more similar to those of re-ordered families than those in low conflict families this does not achieve statistical significance (or anywhere near significance) in this multivariate analysis.

Examining re-ordered family data alone shows exactly similar results to the results outlined above for both main groups combined.

We have postulated that self-esteem, while it may be considered an outcome variable, also appears to be an explanatory variable; linear regression modelling confirms that the only significant explanatory variable for self-esteem is the re-ordered family type. This, together with the fact that it is the most important explanatory variable in the child's data, suggests that the self-esteem score may be an intermediate variable in the analysis. If self-esteem is not entered as a possible explanatory variable, the general picture of the other important explanatory variables is unchanged. This suggests that the influence of re-ordered family type on outcomes for children is not only direct but also has an indirect effect because of its relation to self-esteem.

Data was analysed using linear regression in SPSS and GLIM. In SPSS dummy variables were constructed as necessary to allow analysis of variables with more than two groups.

The Data

Table 1 **The family (parent response)**

	Number of matched pairs	Number reporting problems		Discordant Pairs		Odds Ratio
		Cases C + D	Controls A + C	+I -C (D)	-I +C (A)	
Dissatisfied with housing	76	24	18	18	12	1.5
More than 3 house moves	76	23	6	23	6	3.8**
No car	76	26	10	21	5	4.2**
Financial hardship (Had to go without things)	76	34	16	27	9	3.0***
Currently drawing benefits	76	45	14	33	2	16.5***
Resident Parent's Social Life						
Problems with social life	76	37	29	19	11	1.7
Rarely or never goes out	76	24	44	9	29	0.3**
Marriage						
Dissatisfaction with chores/responsibility						
Now: (Figure 3.2)	76	22	9	20	7	2.9
Past: (Figure 3.3)	76	54	7	51	4	12.8***

Table 2 **Parental health**

	Number of matched pairs	Number reporting problems		Discordant Pairs		Odds Ratio
		Cases C + D	Controls A + C	+I -C (D)	-I +C (A)	
General Health Problems reported by parents						
Not healthy	76	20	11	18	9	2.0
Not satisfied with health care	76	20	9	19	8	2.4*
Problems with nerves now (Figure 3.4)	76	24	6	18	2	9.0***
Problems with nerves past (Figure 3.5)	76	38	10	32	4	8.0***
Smoking and Drinking reported by parents:						
Currently smoking	76	37	16	31	10	3.1*
Smoking in the past	76	43	29	27	13	2.1
Currently drinking	76	64	61	11	8	1.4
Drinking in the past	76	51	44	19	12	1.6
Negative effects of parental health problems on young person reported by parent (Figure 3.6)	76	41	27	25	11	2.3*

Table 3 Problems with "well-being" and self-esteem

	Number of matched pairs	Number reporting problems		Discordant Pairs		Odds Ratio
		Cases C + D	Controls A + C	+I -C (D)	-I +C (A)	
Sometimes/often unhappy						
Reported by: Parents (Figure 4.1)	76	29	11	24	6	4.0**
Young person (Figure 4.2)	74	28	14	23	9	2.6*
Problems with self-esteem (Rosenberg scale)						
Reported by: Young person (Figure 4.3)	74	44	23	28	7	4.0***
Self-Image II						
Reported by young person						2.3***
Social image (Negative):	74	43	28	26	11	
(Affect negative):	74	19	5	16	2	8.0***
Level of responsibility	74	40	32	20	12	1.67
Other people's perception (negative)	74	31	34	15	18	0.83

Table 4 Health problems – parents and child's view

	Number of matched pairs	Number reporting problems		Discordant Pairs		Odds Ratio
		Cases C + D	Controls A + C	+I -C (D)	-I +C (A)	
A) Not healthy						
Reported by: Parent	76	22	13	18	9	2.0
Young person	74	17	7	15	5	3.0*
B) Psychosomatic problems						
Reported by: Parent (Figure 4.8)	76	59	37	29	7	4.1***
Young person	74	64	51	21	8	2.6
C) Psychological Psychiatric/referrals						
Reported by: (Figure 4.9)						
Parent	76	15	5	17	2	8.5***
D) Have you ever stayed in hospital						
Reported by: Young Person	74	41	26	28	13	2.2
E) Number "ever smoked"						
Reported by: Parent	76	6	1	5	0	5.0
Young person	74	18	11	12	5	2.4
Current smoking		4	5	3	4	0.8
F) Number of "ever drank alcohol"						
Reported by: Parent	76	6	1	6	1	6.0
Young person	74	39	23	27	11	2.5**
Current drinking alcohol (Regularly)	74	11	4	9	2	4.5*
G) Of those smoking and drinking currently, do parents know						
Reported by: Young Person	74	33	14	25	6	4.2***

Table 5 **Problems with school reported by child and parent**

		Number of matched pairs	Number reporting problems		Discordant Pairs		Odds Ratio
			Cases C + D	Controls A + C	+I -C (D)	-I +C (A)	
A) General							
a) Not getting on well at school							
Reported by:	Parent	76	15	13	13	11	1.2
	Young Person	74	32	26	17	11	1.5
b) Truancy or refusal							
Reported by:	Parent	76	20	10	16	6	2.7
	Young Person	74	13	9	12	8	1.5
c) Not wanting to go to school							
Reported by:	Young Person	74	48	40	22	14	1.6
B) Academic							
a) Difficulties with school work ("Ever")							
Reported by:	Parent	76	38	25	25	12	2.1
	Young Person (Figure 4.10)	74	38	26	20	17	2.9*
b) Had extra help with school work							
Reported by:	Parent (Figure 4.11)	76	31	14	24	7	3.4**
	Young Person	74	27	15	22	10	2.2
C) Relationships in school							
a) Difficulties with teachers							
Reported by:	Parents	76	25	23	21	19	1.1
	Young Person	74	30	23	23	16	1.4
b) Difficulties with friends							
Reported by:	Parents	76	35	31	23	19	1.2
	Young Person	74	32	20	22	10	2.2
c) Extra changes of school							
Reported by:	Parent (Figure 4.12)	76	39	22	24	7	3.4**
	Young Person	74	33	21	20	8	2.5*

The Exeter Family Study

Table 6 **The child's social life**

		Number of matched pairs	Number reporting problems		Discordant Pairs		Odds Ratio
			Cases C + D	Controls A + C	+I -C (D)	-I +C (A)	
A) Dissatisfied with social life							
Reported by:	Parent	76	32	12	29	9	3.2**
	Young Person	74	27	14	22	9	2.4*
B) Too few friends							
Reported by:	Parent	76	22	20	20	8	2.5*
	Young Person	74	24	15	19	10	1.9
C) Problems with Friends							
Reported by:	Young Person (Figure 4.15)	74	26	19	17	10	1.7
D) Worries about friendships							
Reported by:	Parent (Figure 4.16)	76	37	22	28	13	2.2*
E) Constraints on child's social life							
Reported by:	Parent	76	32	25	18	11	1.6
	Young Person	74	22	16	16	10	1.6
F) Changes about bringing friends home							
Reported by:	Parent	76	23	3	22	2	11.0*
	Young Person	74	15	3	13	1	13.0*

Table 7 **The child's mood and behaviour**

	Number of matched pairs	Number reporting problems		Discordant Pairs		Odds Ratio
		Cases C + D	Controls A + C	+I -C (D)	-I +C (A)	
Behaviour upsets other people reported by child:						
(Figure 4.20)	74	51	36	26	11	2.4
Child's behaviour upsetting to parents						
Parent's view (Figure 4.19)	76	47	29	27	9	3**
Friends behaviour upsetting						
	74	16	17	11	12	0.9
Other family members behaviour (sibs, grandparents, etc) upsetting	74	31	17	25	11	2.3
Teachers/authority figures (problems)	74	10	4	9	3	3.0
Negative changes in mood (approximately over last year or since separation/ divorce reported by family						
(Figure 4.17)	76	44	27	28	11	2.5**
Negative changes in behaviour (approximately over last year or since separation/divorce reported by family	76	25	8	21	4	5.3***

Table 8 Children and their parents

	Number of matched pairs	Number reporting problems		Discordant Pairs		Odds Ratio
		Cases C + D	Controls A + C	+I -C (D)	-I +C (A)	
A) Major disagreements between carer parent and child						
Reported by: Parent (Figure 4.21)	76	19	10	15	6	2.9**
Young Person	74	14	12	14	12	1.2
B) No discussion about personal relationships						
Reported by: Parent	76	11	14	9	12	0.8
Young Person	74	35	46	12	23	0.5
C) No regular family outings						
Reported by: Parent (Figure 4.23)	76	51	38	25	12	2.1
D) Unreasonable expectations						
Reported by: Parent (Figure 4.22)	76	30	16	24	10	2.4
E) Independence						
a) Father does "unnecessary" things for child						
Reported by: Child	74	4	9	4	9	0.4
b) Mother does "Unnecessary" things for child						
Reported by: Child	74	19	12	17	10	1.7

Table 9 Contact and support – carer relatives

	Number of matched pairs	Number reporting problems		Discordant Pairs		Odds Ratio
		Cases C + D	Controls A + C	+I -C (D)	-I +C (A)	
Contact non-resident parent grandparents less than once a month						
(Figure 4.25)	76	29	26 (mat)	18	15	1.2
Contact non-resident parent grandparents less than once a month						
(Figure 4.26)	76	55	37 (pat)	29	11	2.6**
Little support for child from resident parent grandparents						
(Figure 4.27)	76	21	10 (mat)	19	8	2.4*
Little support for child from non-resident parent grandparents						
(Figure 4.29)	76	50	21 (pat)	40	11	3.6***
Little support for parent from resident parent grandparents						
(Figure 4.28)	76	22	12 (mat)	20	10	2.0
Little support for parent from non-resident parent grandparent	76	51	24 (pat)	36	9	4.0***
Change in contact with relatives reported by young person						
(Figure 4.24)	74	59	22	41	4	10.3***

Table 10 **Expectations and the future**

	Number of matched pairs	Number reporting problems		Discordant Pairs		Odds Ratio
		Cases C + D	Controls A + C	+I -C (D)	-I +C (A)	
A) Uncertain about future						
a) for family reported by parents:	76	46	40	21	15	1.4
b) for child reported by parent:	74	32	24	20	12	1.7
B) Marriage						
a) Would you like to get married?	74	33	29	17	13	1.3
b) Do you think you will get married?	74	27	24	18	15	1.2
C) Children						
a) Wouldn't like to have children in the future?	74	7	14	5	12	0.4

Department of Child Health

University of Exeter

Self-Esteem Rating

Yes	–	1
No	–	2
Yes, but hesitates	–	3
No, but hesitates	–	4

1   Most of the time I'm good fun to be with ☐

2   I often think things are too much for me ☐

3   People often make fun of me ☐

4   It takes a long time for others to accept me ☐

5   I often feel happy ☐

6   I'm very uncomfortable in the company of strangers ☐

7   People usually take notice of what I say ☐

8   I am often worried about my appearance ☐

9   In groups of people I often feel the odd one out ☐

10 Other people depend on me ☐

11 I worry a lot about what other people think of me ☐

12 Sometimes I think I am more capable of doing things than other people ☐

13 I often feel lonely ☐

14 The way other people treat me often makes me angry ☐

15 I take responsibility for myself ☐

16 Other people often decide things for me ☐

17 I often feel miserable ☐

18 Sometimes I feel I have to work harder than anyone else to prove how good I am ☐

19 I often feel life is not worth living ☐

20 On the whole I cope well with life ☐

21 On the whole I am satisfied with life ☐

22 I don't usually worry about what other people think of me ☐

Bibliography

Ahrons, S.C.R. & Rodgers, R. (1987) *Divorced Families: A Multi-disciplinary Developmental View.* Norton

Ainsworth, M.D.S. (1979) Infant mother attachment. *American Psychologist* **34**, 932–937

Allison, P.D. & Furstenberg, F.F. Jr (1989) How marital dissolution affects children: variations by age and sex. *Developmental Psychology* **25**, 540–549

Amato, P. (1987) Childrens' reactions to parental separation and divorce: the views of children and custodial mothers. *Australian Journal of Social Issues* **22**(4), 610–623

Amato, P. (1993) Children's adjustment to divorce: theories, hypotheses, and emperical support. *Journal of Marriage and the Family* 23–38

Amato, P. & Bruce, K. (1991) Parental divorce and the well-being of children: a meta-analysis. *Psychological Bulletin* **110**(1), 26–46

Bank, S. & Kahan, M.D. (1982) *The Sibling Bond.* Basic Books (New York)

Bebbington, A. & Miles, J. (1989) The background of children who enter local authority care. *British Journal of Social Work* **19**,5

Block, J.H, Block, J.G., & Jerde, P.F. (1986) The personality of children prior to divorce. A prospective study. *Child Development* **57**, 827–840

Bowlby, J. (1979) *The Making and Breaking of Affectional Bonds.* Tavistock (London)

Bowlby, J. (1982) *Attachment and Loss. 1: Attachment.* Basic Books (New York)

Bradshaw, J. & Millar, J. (1991) *Lone Parent Families in the UK.* Department of Social Security Report 6, HMSO (London)

Brimblecombe, F.S.W. (1987) The voice of disabled young people – the Exeter project. *Children and Society* **1**, 58–70

Bumpass, L. (1984) Children in marital disruption: a replication and update. *Demography* **21**,71–82

Burghes, L. (1993). *Lone Parents: Policy Options for the 90s.* Joseph Rowntree Foundation, Family Policy Studies Centre (London)

Burgoyne, J. & Clark, D. (1984) *Making a Go of It: A Study of Step-families in Sheffield.* Routledge & Kegan Paul (London)

Burgoyne, J., Ormrod, R. & Richards, M. (1987) *Divorce Matters.* Penguin Books (Harmondsworth)

Butler, N.R. & Golding, J. (1986) *From Birth To Five: A Study Of The Health And Behaviour Of Britain's Five Year Olds.* Pergamon (Oxford)

Camara, K.A. (1981) Children of divorce: Cognitive and social functioning. Department of Health and Human Services/ National Institute of Mental Health (Bethesda, MD)

Camara, K.A. & Resnick, G. (1988) Interparental conflict and co-operation: factors moderating children's post divorce adjustment. In: E.M. Hetherington and J.D. Arasteh (Eds) *Impact of divorce, single parenting and step parenting on children: 169-196.* Erlbaum, Hillsdale NJ.

Camara, K.A., Weiss. R., & Hess R.D. (1981) *Remarried fathers and their children.* Paper presented at the biennial meeting of the Society in Child Development

Capaldi, D.M. (1989) *The relation of family transitions and disruptions to boys' adjustment problems.* Paper presented at the conference of the Society for Research in Child Development, Kansas City, MO.

Capaldi, D.M. & Patterson, G.R. (1987) An approach to the problem of recruitment rates for longitudinal research. *Behavioral Assessment* **9**,169–178

Capaldi, D.M. & Patterson, G.R. (1989) *Psychometric Properties of Fourteen Latent Constructs from the Oregon Youth Study.* Springer-Verlag (New York)

Capaldi, D. M. & Patterson, G.R. (1991) Relation of parental transitions to boys' adjustment problems: I, A linear hypothesis. II, Mothers at risk for transitions and unskilled parenting. *Developmental Psychology,* **27**(3), 489–504.

Capron, D. (1994) *A Review of 1992.* Population Trends 75, HMSO (London)

Chase-Lansdale, P.L. & Hetherington, E.M. (1990) The impact of divorce on life-span development: short- and long-term effects. In D.L. Featherman & R.M. Lerner (Eds) *Life-span development and behavior,* 105–150. Lawrence Erlbaum (Hillsdale, NJ)

Cherlin, A.J. (1978). Remarriage as an incomplete institution. *American Journal of Sociology* **84**, 634–650

Cherlin, A.J. (1981) *Marriage, divorce, and remarriage.* Harvard University Press

Cherlin, A.J. & Furstenberg, F.F. Jr (1986) *The New American Grandparent.* Basic Books (New York)

Cherlin, A.J. & McCarthy, J. (1985) Remarried couple households: data from the June 1980 current population survey. *Journal of Marriage and the Family* **47**, 23–30

Cherlin, A.J., Furstenberg, F., Chase-Lansdale, L. & Kiernan, K. (1991) *Longitudinal studies of effects of divorce on children in Great Britain and the United States. The effects of divorce on children's emotional adjustment: five perspective studies.* Paper presented at the meeting of the Society for Research in Child Development, Seattle

Chester, R. (1973) Health and marital breakdown: some implications for doctors. *Journal of Psychosomatic Research* **17**(4), 317–321

Clark, D., Cuthill, A., McPhearson, J. & Manson, D. *Divorce and the School,* 197–216

Cockett, M., Kuh, D. & Tripp, J.H. (1986) *Bridges Over Troubled Waters*. Report for the Health Advisory Service

Cockett, M., Kuh, D., & Tripp, J. H. (1987) The needs of disturbed adolescents. *Children and Society* **2**, 93–113

Cummings, E.M., Zahn-Waxler, C. & Radke-Yarrow, M. (1984) Developmental changes in children's reactions to anger in the home. *Journal of Child Psychology and Psychiatry* **25**, 63–74

Curtis, H. A., Tripp, J. H., Lawrence, C. & Clarke, W. (1988) Teenage relationships and sex education. *Archives of Diseases in Childhood* **63**, 935–941

Davis, G. & Murch, M. (1988) *Grounds for Divorce*. Oxford University Press

Davis, G. & Roberts, M. (1989) Mediation in disputes over children: learning from experience. *Children and Society*, 275–279

Dominian, J., Mansfield, P., Dormor, D. & McAllister, F. (1991) *Marital Breakdown and the Health of the Nation*. One plus One

Douglas, J.W.B. (1970) Broken homes and child behaviour. *Journal of the Royal College of Physicians (London)* **4**, 203–210

Douglas, J.W.B. (1973) Early disturbing events and later enuresis. In I. Kolvin, R.C. McKeith & S.R. Meadow (Eds) *Bladder Control and Enuresis*. Spastics International Medical (London)

Dunlop, R. & Burns, A. (1983) *Adolescents and divorce: the experience of family break-up*. Proceedings of the Australian Family Research Conference. II, Family Law. Australian Institute of Family Studies (Melbourne)

Dunlop, R. & Burns, A. (1988) *Don't Feel the World is Caving In: Adolescents in Divorcing Families*, Monograph No. 6. Australian Institute of Family Studies (Melbourne)

Eekelaar, J. (1991a) A child support scheme for the United Kingdom – an analysis of the White Paper. *Family Law*, **21**, 15–21

Eekelaar, J. (1991b) Child support – an evaluation. *Family Law*, **21**, 511–517

Eekelaar, J. & MacLean, M. (1986) *Maintenance after Divorce*. Oxford University Press

Elliot, J. & Richards, M.P.M. (1991) Children and divorce: educational performance and behaviour before and after parental separation. *International Journal of Law and the Family*, **5**: 258–276

Emery, R.E. (1988) Family processes and children's adjustment. *Marriage Divorce and Children's Adjustment* **14**, 71–116

Erikson, S. & McKnight, M. (1990) Mediating spousal abuse divorces. *Mediation Quarterly* **7**(4), 377–388

Fergusson, D.M., Dimond, M.E. & Horwood, L.J. (1986) Childhood family, placement history and behaviour problems in 6 year old children. *Journal of Child Psychology and Psychiatry* **27**, 213–226

Ferri, E. (1976). *Growing Up in a One Parent Family: A Long Term Study of Child Development*. National Foundation for Educational Research Publishing (Berkshire, UK)

Ferri, E. (1984) *Step children; a National Study*. National Foundation for Educational Research. Nelson, England.

Ferri, E. et al. (1993) *Life at 33 – The Fifth Follow-up of the National Child Development Study*. National Children's Bureau, 8 Wakeley Street, London, England.

Finch, J. (1989) *Family Obligations and Social Change*. Polity Press. England.

Finch, J. & Mason, J. (1993) *Negotiating Family Responsibilities*. Routledge

Fisher, T. (1987) *Towards a Model for Co-working in Family Conciliation*, 365–382. British Association of Social Workers

Folberg, J. (1984). *Joint custody and shared parenting*. BNA (Washington D.C.)

Fry, P.S. & Addington, J. (1984) Professionals' negative expectations of boys from father-headed, single parent families: implications for the training of child care professionals. *British Journal of Developmental Psychology* **2**, 337–346

Furstenberg F.F. Jr (1979) Recycling the family; perspectives for researching a neglecte d family form. *Marriage and Family Review* **2**(3), 2–22

Furstenberg, F.F. Jr (1981) *Re-negotiating parenthood after divorce and remarriage*. Paper presented at the Biennial meeting of the Society for Research in Child Development, Symposium on Changing Family Patterns, Boston, MA

Furstenberg, F.F. Jr (1982) Conjugal succession: re-entering marriage after divorce. *Life span development and behavior* **4**, 107–145

Furstenberg, F.F. Jr (1987) The new extended family: the experience of parents and children after remarriage. In K. Pasley & M. Ihinger-Tallman (Eds). *Remarriage and step-parenting: Current Research and Theory*, 42–61 Guildford Press (New York)

Furstenberg, F.F. Jr (1988) Child care after divorce and remarriage. In E.M. Hetherington & J. Aresteh (Eds) *Impact of Divorce, Single Parenting and Step Parenting on Children*, 245–262. Lawrence Erlbaum (Hillsdale, NJ)

Furstenberg, F.F. Jr & Allison, P.D. (1985). *How marital dissolution affects children: variations by age and sex.* Unpublished manuscript, University of Pennsylvania

Furstenberg, F.F. Jr & Cherlin, A.J. (1991) (Eds) *Divided Families: The Family and Public Policy*. Harvard Press. USA

Furstenberg, F.F. Jr & Nord, C.W. (1985) Parenting apart: patterns of childrearing after marital disruption. *Journal of Marriage and the Family* **47**, 893–904

Furstenberg, F.F. Jr & Spanier, S.B. (1984) *Recycling the Family Remarriage after Divorce*. Sage Publications (Beverley Hills)

Furstenberg, F.F. Jr, Nord, C.W., Peterson, J.L. & Zill, N. (1983) The life course of children of divorce: marital dissolution and parental contact. *American Sociologicial Review*, **48**(5), 656–668

Furstenberg F.F. Jr, Morgan, S.P. & Allison, P.D. (1987) *Paternal participation and children's well-being after marital separation*. Paper presented at the Annual Meeting of the Population Association of America, Chicago

The Exeter Family Study

Ganong, L.H. & Coleman, M.M. Stepchildren's perceptions of their parents. *Genetic Psychology* **148**(1), 5017

Goodyer, I. (1990) Family relationships, life events and childhood psychopathology. *Journal of Child Psychology and Psychiatry* **31**(1), 161–192

Goodyer, I. (1992) Stressful life events and childhood illnesses. *Archives of Diseases in Childhood*, **6 No 7**, 673–674

Guidubaldi, J., Cleminshaw, H.K., Perry, J.D. & McLoughlin, C.S. (1983) The impact of parental divorce on children: Report of the nationwide NASP study. *School Psychology Review* **12**, 300–323

Guidubaldi, J., Perry, J.D. & Cleminshaw, H.K. (1984) The legacy of parental divorce: A nationwide study of family status and selected mediating variables on children's academic and social competencies. *Advances in Child Clinical Psychology* **7**, 109–155

Guidubaldi, J., Perry, J.D. & Nastasi, B.K. (1987) Growing up in a divorced family: initial and long-term perspectives on children's adjustment. In S. Oskamp (Ed), *Applied social psychology annual. 7: Family processes and problems*, 202–237. Sage Publications (Beverley Hills)

Hagestad, G.O. (1985) *Continuity and Connectedness in Grand-Parenthood*. Sage Publications

Harty, M. & Wood, J. (1991) From shared care to shared residence. *Family Law*, **21**, 430–433

Haynes, M. & Haynes, G. (1989) *Mediating Divorce*. Jossey Bass (San Francisco)

Hernandez, D.J. (1988) Demographic trends and the living arrangements of children. In E.M. Hetherington & J.D. Arasteh (eds), *Impact of Divorce, Single Parenting, and Stepparenting on Children*, 3–22. Lawrence Erlbaum (Hillsdale, NJ)

Hess, R.D. & Camara, K.A. (1979). Post-divorce family relationships as mediating factors in the consequences of divorce for children. *Journal of Personality and Social Psychology* **4**, 87–91.

Hestor, M. & Radford, L. (1992) Domestic violence and access arrangements for children in Denmark and Britain. *Journal of Social Welfare and Family Law* **1**, 57–70

Hetherington, E.M. (1987) Family relations six years after divorce. In K. Pasley & M. Ihinger-Tallman (Eds), *Remarriage and Step-parenting Today: Research and Theory*, 185–205. Guildford Press (New York)

Hetherington, E.M. & Arastek, J.D. (Eds) (1988) *Impact of Divorce, Single Parenting and Step Parenting on Children*, 169–196. Lawrence Erlbaum (Hillsdale NJ)

Hetherington, E.M. & Camara, K.A. (1984) Families in transition: The processes of dissolution and reconstitution. In R.D. Parke (Ed), *Review of child development research. 7: The family*. University of Chicago Press

Hetherington, E.M. & Camara, K.A. (1988) The effects of family dissolution and reconstitution on children. In N.D. Glenn & M.T. Coleman (Eds), *Family Relations: A Reader*, 420–431. Dorsey Press (Chicago)

Hetherington, E.M., Cox, M. & Cox, R. (1979) Stress and coping in divorce: a focus on women. In J. Gullahorn (Ed), *Psychology of Women in Transition*, 95–128. B.H.Winston & Sons (Washington DC)

Hetherington, E.M., Cox, M. & Cox, R. (1981) Effects of divorce on parents and children. In M. Lamb (Ed), *Nontraditional Families*, 233–288. Lawrence Erlbaum (Hillsdale, NJ)

Hetherington, E.M., Cox, M. & Cox, R. (1985) Long-term effects of divorce and remarriage on the adjustment of children. *Journal of the American Academy of Child Psychiatry* **24**(5), 518–530

Hetherington, E.M., Clingempeel, W.G. et al. (1992) *Coping with Marital Transitions. Family System Perspective*. Monograph of the Society for Research in Child Development. Serial No 227, 57

Hirst, S.R. & Smiley, G.W. (1984) The access dilemma – a study of access patterns following marriage breakdown. *Conciliation Courts Review* **22**(1), 41–52

Hodges, W.F. (1986) *Interventions for Children of Divorce*. Wiley Inter-science. USA.

Hodges, W.F., Buchsbaum, H.K. & Tierney, C.W. (1983) Parent–child relationships and adjustment in pre-school children in divorced and intact families. *Journal of Divorced and Intact Families/Journal of Marriage and the Family* **46**, 611–617

Hoghughi, M. (1992) *Assessing Child and Adolescent Disorders*. Sage Publications (Beverley Hills)

Holmes, T.H. & Rahe, R.H. (1967) The Holmes–Rahe Social Readjustment Ratings Scale. *Journal of Psychosomatic Research*, **11**, 213-218

Hunter, J.E. & Schuman, (1980) Chronic reconstitution as a family style. *Social Work* **6**, 446–451

Jacobs, J.A. & Furstenberg, F.F. Jr (1986) Changing places: conjugal careers and woman's marital morbidity. *Social Forces* **64**, 714–732

Jacobs, N.L., Guidubaldi, J. & Nastasi, B. (1986) Adjustment of divorce-family day care children. *Early Childhood Research Quarterly* **1**, 361–378

Jenkins, J.M. & Smith, M.A. (1990) Factors protecting children in disharmonious homes: maternal reports. *American Academy of Child and Adolescent Psychiatry* **29**(1), 60–69

Jenkins, J.M. & Smith, M.A. (1991) Marital disharmony and children's behaviour problems: aspects of a poor marriage that affect children adversely. *Journal of Child Psychology and Psychiatry* **32**(5), 793–810

Johnson, A.J.R., Campbell, L.E.G. & Mayse. S.S. (1985) latency children in post-separation and divorce disputes. *Journal of the American Academy of Child Psychiatry* **24**(5)

Jones, P. (1991) The Child Support Act: In the best interests of the child? Comment. *Family Law*, 451

Kalter, N. (1987) Long-term effects of divorce on children: a developmental vulnerability model. *American Journal of Orthopsychiatry* **57**(4), 587–600

Kalter, N. & Rembar, J. (1981) The significance of a child's age at the time of parental divorce. *American Journal of Orthopsychiatry* **51**, 85–100

Kalter, N., Kloner, A., Schreier, S., & Okla, K. (1989) Predictors of children's post divorce adjustment. *American Journal of Orthopsychiatry*, **59**, 605–620

Kalter, N. et al. (1993) *Time-limited developmental facilitation groups for children of divorce: early adolescent manual.* Unpublished manuscript

Karen, R. (1994) *Becoming Attached: Unfolding the Mystery of the Infant–Mother Bond and its Impact on Later Life.* Warner Books (New York)

Kelly, J.B. (1991) Mediated and adversarial divorce resolution processes – a comparison of post-divorce outcomes. *Family Law*, 382–388

Kelly, J.B. (1981) The visiting relationship after divorce: research findings and clinical implications. In I.R. Stuart & L.E. Abt (Eds), *Children of Separation and Divorce - Management and Treatment*, 338–361. Van Nostrand Reinhold (New York)

Kelly, J.B. (1982a) Divorce: The adult perspective. In B. Wolman & G. Stricker (Eds), *Handbook of Developmental Psychology*, 734–750. Prentice-Hall (Englewood Cliffs)

Kelly, J.B. (1982b) Observations on adolescent relationships five years after divorce. In S. Feinstein (Ed), *Adolescent Psychiatry*, 133–141. University of Chicago Press

Kiernan, K.E. (1986) Teenage marriage and marital breakdown: a longitudinal study. *Population Studies*, **40**(1):35

Kiernan, K.E. (1991) *The impact of family disruption in childhood on transitions made in young adult life.* Paper presented Population Association of America annual meeting, Washington D.C.

Kiernan, K.E. (1992) The impact of family disruption in childhood on transitions made in young adult life. *Population Studies* **46**,213-234

Kiernan, K.E. & Chase-Lansdale P. (1991) Children and marital breakdown: short and long-term consequences. In *Proceedings of the European Demographic Conference.*

Kiernan, K.E. & Estaugh, V. (1993) *Cohabitation. Extra-marital Child-bearing and Social Policy.* Family Policy Studies Centre (London)

Kiernan, K.E. & Wicks, M. (1990) *Family Change and Future Policy.* Family Policy Studies Centre (London)

Kuh, D. & Maclean, M. (1990) Women's childhood experience of parental separation and their subsequent health and socio-economic status in adulthood. *Journal of Biosocial Science* **22**, 121–135

Kurdek, L.A. & Berg, B. (1983) Correlates of children's adjustment to their parent's divorces. In L.A. Kurdek (Ed), *Children and Divorce: New directions for child development* (No. 19). Jossey-Bass (San Francisco)

Kurdek, L.A., Blisk, D. & Seisky, A.E. (1981) Correlates of children's long term adjustment to their parent's divorce. *Developmental Psychology* **17**, 565–579

Lord Chancellor's Department (1993) *Looking to the Future. Mediation and the Ground for Divorce – A Consultative Paper.* HMSO (London)

Luepnitz, D.A. (1982) *Child Custody: A study of families after Divorce.* Lexington Books. USA

Lutz, P. (1983) The step-family: an adolescent perspective. *Family Relations* **32**, 367–375

Maclean, M. & Eekelaar, J. (1983) *Children and Divorce.* Oxford University/Centre for Socio-Legal Studies

Maclean, M. & Wadsworth, M.E.J. (1988) The interests of children after parental divorce; a long-term perspective. *International Journal of Law and the Family*, **2**,155-166

Mansfield, P. & Collard, J. (1988) *The Beginning of the Rest of your Life.* Macmillan. England.

Marriage and Divorce Statistics (1989) OPCS. Series FM2. No. 17, HMSO (London)

McCormick, A. & Rosenbaum, M. (1990) *Morbidity Statistics for General Practice: Third National Study.* HMSO (London)

McLanahan, S.S. (1985) Family structure and reproduction of parenting. *American Journal of Sociology* **90**, 875–901

McLanahan, S.S. (1988). Family structure and dependency: early transitions to female household headship. *Demography*, **25**, 1–15

McLanahan, S.S. & Bumpass, L. (1988). Inter-generational consequences of family disruption. *American Journal of Sociology*, **94**,130–152

McLoughlin, D. & Whitefield, R. (1984) Adolescents and their experience of parental divorce. *Journal of Adolescence* **7**, 155–170

McNemar, (1962) *Psychological Tests.* Wiley (Chichester)

McRae, S. (1993). *Changing Marriage and Motherhood?* Policy Studies Institute (753) London

Mechanic, D. & Hansell, S. (1989) Divorce, family, conflict, and adolescents' well-being. *Journal of Health and Social Behaviour* **30**, 105–116

Mitchell, A. (1985) *Children in the Middle. Living Through Divorce*, 1–191. Tavistock (London)

Morrison, J.R. (1974) Parental divorce as a factor in childhood psychiatric illness. *Comprehensive Psychiatry* **15**, 95–102

Newcomer, S. & Udry, J.R. (1987) Parental marital status effects on adolescent sexual behavior. *Journal of Marriage and the Family* **49**, 235–240

Office of Population, Censuses and Surveys (1989) *Marriage and Divorce Statistics*, Series 00, No. 00. HMSO (London)

Ourth, J. (1980) Children in one-parent homes: the school factor. *Principal* **60**(1), 40

Ourth, J. & Zakariya, S.B. (1982) The school and the single-parent student: what schools can do to help. *Principal*, **62**(1), 24–26, 31, 38

Packman, J. (1986) Social work decisions in child care: recent researcxh findings and their implications. HMSO(London)

Parish, T. & Dostal, J. (1980) Evaluations of self and parent figures by children from intact, divorced, and reconstituted families. *Journal of Youth and Adolescence*, **9**, 347–351

Parish, T. (1981) Concordance of children's descriptions of themselves and their parents as a function of intact versus divorced families. *Journal of Psychology* **107**, 199–201

Parish, T. & Wigle, S. (1985) A longitudinal study of the impact of divorce on adolescents' evaluation of self and parents. *Adolescence* **20**, 239–244

Parkinson, L. (1986) *Conciliation in Separation and Divorce.* Croom Helm. England

Parkinson, L. (1991) The Split Couple: Conciliation and Mediation Approaches, in D. Hooper & W. Dryden (Eds), *Couple Therapy – A Handbook*, 217–237. Open University Press

Parkinson, L. (1987) *Separation, Divorce And Families. Practical Social Work*. Macmillan Education. England

Pasley, K. & Ihinger-Tallman, M. (1987) *Remarriage and Step-parenting: Current Research and Theory*. Guildford Press (New York)

Pearson, J. (1989) *Divorce: American Mediation Research* (Conference Address). School of Social Work, University of Bath

Pearson, J. (1991) The equity of mediated divorce agreements. *Mediation Quarterly* 9, 179

Pearson, J. (1993). Ten myths about family law. *Family Quarterly*, 27(2)

Pearson, J. & Thoeness, N. (1982) The mediation and adjudication of divorce disputes; some costs and benefits. *The Family Advocate* 4, 26–32

Pearson, J. & Thoennes, N. (1988a) Reflections on a decade of divorce mediation in mediation research: The process and effectiveness of third party intervention. In K.K. Kressel et al. (Eds), 9–30

Pearson, J. & Thoeness, N. (1988b) Divorce mediation: research results in divorce mediation. *In Theory and practice*, (Eds) J. Folberg, J.A. Milne 429

Peterson, J, & Zill, N. (1986) Marital disruption, parent/child relationships and behaviour problems in children. *Journal of Marriage and the Family* 48, 295–307

Phinney, V.G. Jensen, L.C., Olsen, J.A. & Cundick, B. (1990) The relationship between early development and psychosexual behaviors in adolescent females. *Adolescence* 25(98), 322–331

Quinton, D. & Rutter, M. (1985) *Family Pathology and Child Psychiatric Disorder; A Four-Year Prospective Study*. John Wiley & Sons Ltd (Chichester) England

Quinton, D. & Rutter, M. (1988) *Parental Breakdown: The Making and Breaking of Intergenerational Links*. Gower. England

Raschke, J.H. & Raschke, V.J. (1979) Family conflict and children's self-concepts: a comparison of intact and single-parent families. *Journal of Marriage and the Family* 41, 367–374

Richards, M.P.M. (Eds) (1974) *The Integration of a Child into a Social World*. Cambridge University Press

Richards, M.P.M. (1982a) Post-divorce arrangements for children: A psychological perspective. *Journal of Social Welfare Law*, 69,133–151

Richards, M.P.M. (1982b) Marital separation and children: some problems of method and theory. *International Journal of Sociology and Social Policy*, 2, 75–84

Richards, M.P.M. (1987) Children, parents and families; developmental psychology and the re-ordering of relationships at divorce. *International Journal of Law and the Family*, 295–317

Richards, M.P.M. (1988) Development psychology and family law: A discussion paper. *British Journal of Developmental Psychology*, 6, 169-181

Richards, M.P.M. (1991) The effects of parental divorce on children. *Archives of Diseases in Childhood*, 66, 915-916

Roberts, M. (1988) *Mediation in Family Disputes: Modern Lw Review:* 46(5)

Robinson, M. & Smith, D. (1993) *Step by Step. Focus on Step-families*. Harvester Wheatsheaf (Hemel Hempstead)

Rosenberg, M. (1965) *Variant Family Forms.*

Rosenberg, M. (1979) *Conceiving the Self*. Basic Books (New York)

Rutter, M. (1971) Parent–child separation: psychological effects on the children. *Journal of Child Psychology and Psychiatry* 12, 233–260

Rutter, M. (1976). Adolescent turmoil, fact or fiction. *Journal of Child Psychology and Psychiatry*, 17, 35–56.

Rutter, M. (1981) *Maternal Deprivation Re-assessed* (2nd ed) Penguin (Harmondsworth)

Rutter, M. (1985) Family and school influences on behavioural development. *Journal of Child Psychology and Psychiatry* 16, 683–704

Rutter, M. (1989a) Resilience in the face of adversity: protective factors and re sistance to psychiatric disorders. *British Journal of Psychiatry* 147, 598–611

Rutter, M. (1989b) Pathways from childhood to adult life. *Journal of Childhood Psychology and Psychiatry* 30(1) 23–51

Rutter, M. (1991) *Pathways from childhood to adult life: the role of schooling*. Westminster School Lecture

Santrock, J.W. & Sitterle, K. (1987) Families in transition. In K. Pasley & M. Ihinger-Tallman (Eds), *Remarriage and Parenting*, 273-299. Guildford Press (New York)

Santrock, J.W. & Tracey, R.L. (1978) The effects of children's family structure status on the development of stereotypes by teachers. *Journal of Educational Psychology* 70, 754–757

Santrock, J.W. & Warshak, R (1979) Father custody and social development in boys and girls. *Journal of Social Issues* 35, 112–125

Santrock, J.W., Warshak, R.A. & Elliott, G.L. (1982a) Social development and parent-child interaction in father-custody and stepmother families. In M.E. Lamb (Ed), *Non-traditional Families: Parenting and Child Development*. Lawrence Erlbaum (Hillsdale NJ)

Santrock, J.W., Warshak, R., Lindbergh, C. & Meadows, L. (1982b) Children's and parents' observed social behavior in stepfather families. *Child Development* 53, 472–480

Schaffer, H.R. (1990) *Making Decisions about Children: Psychological Questions and Answers*. Blackwell. Cambridge, Mass., USA.

Shinn, M. (1978) Father absence and children's cognitive development. *Psychological Bulletin* 85, 295–324

Slater, E.J. & Haber J.D. (1984) Adolescent adjustment following divorce as a function of family conflict. *Journal of Consulting and Clinical Psychology* 52, 920–921

Smith, M.A. & Jenkins, J.M. (1991) The effects of marital disharmony on pre-pubertal children. *Journal of Abnormal Child Psychology* 19, 625–644

Touliatos, J. & Lindholm, B. (1980) Teachers perceptions of behaviour problems in children from intact, single parent and step-parent families. *Psychology in the Schools* **17**, 264–269

Van Bueren, G. (1992) The United Nations Convention on the rights of the child – the necessity of incorporation into UK Law. *Family Law*, **22**, 373–375

Visher, E.B. & Visher, J.S. (1979) *Step-families: A Guide to Working with Step-parents and Step-children*. Brunner/Maxel (New York)

Visher, E.B. & Visher, J.S. (1985) Step-families are different. *Journal of Family Therapy* **7**, 9–18

Visher, E.B. & Visher J.S. (1988) Treating families with problems associated with remarriage and step-relationships. In C.S. Chilman, E.W. Nunnelly & F.M. Cox (Eds), *Variant Family Forms*. Sage Publications (Beverley Hills)

Wadsworth, M.E.J. (1987) Follow up of the First National Birth cohort. *Paediatric and Perinatal Epidemiology* **1**, 95–117

Wadsworth, M.E.J. (1988) The interests of children after parental divorce: a long term perspective. *International Journal of Law and the Family* **2**, 155–166

Wadsworth, M.E.J. (1991) *The Imprint of Time. Childhood History and Adult Life*. Clarendon Press (Oxford)

Wadsworth, M.E.J. & Maclean, M. (1986) *Parents' Divorce and Children's Life Chances*, Children and Youth Services Review, **8**:145-159

Wadsworth, M.E.J., MacLean, M., Kuh, D. & Rogers, B. (1990) Children of divorced and separated parents: summary of review findings from a long term follow up in the UK. *Family Practice* **7**(1) 104-109

Walker et al. (1989) *Cost and Effectiveness of Family Conciliation*. Lord Chancellor's Department (London)

Wallerstein, J.S. (1984) Children of divorce: preliminary report of a ten year following of young children. *American Journal of Orthopsychiatry* **54**(3), 444–458

Wallerstein, J.S. (1988) Children of divorce. *Stress and Developmental Tasks* **2**, 265–302

Wallerstein, J.S. & Blakeslee, S. (1989) *Second Chances: Men Women & Children – A Decade After Divorce*. Tickner Fields, New York, USA

Wallerstein, J.S. & Corbin, S.B. (1986) Father–child relationships after divorce: support and educational opportunity. *Family Law Quarterly* **20**, 109–129

Wallerstein, J.S. & Kelly, J.B. (1980) *Surviving the Breakup: How Children and Parents Cope with Divorce*. Grant McIntyre (London)

Wallerstein, J.S., Corbin, S.B. & Lewis, J.M. (1988) Children of divorce: a ten year study. In E.M. Hetherington & J.D. Arasteh (Eds), *Impact of Divorce, Single Parenting and Step-parenting on Children,* 198–214. Lawrence Erlbaum (Hillsdale, NJ)

Walzak, Y. & Burns, S. (1984) *Divorce, The Child's Point of View*. Harper & Row (London)

Warshak, R.A. & Santrock, J.W. (1993) Children of divorce: Impact of custody disposition on social development. In E.J. Callahan & K.A. McCluskey (Eds), *Life-span Developmental Psychology: Non-normative Life Events*, 241–263. Academic Press (New York)

Watt, N., Moorehead-Slaughter, O., Japzon, D. & Keller, G. (1989) Children's adjustment to parental divorce: self image, social relations and school performance. In J. Rolfe et al. (Eds), *Risk and Protective Factors Development of Psychopathology*. Cambridge University Press

Weiss, R. (1975) *Marital Separation*. Basic Books (New York)

Weiss, R. (1984) *Divorce – The Child's Point of View*. Harper & Row (London)

White, L.K. & Booth, A. (1985) Step-children in remarriages. *American Sociological Review* **50**, 689–698

Wicks, M. (1989) Family Trends, Insecurities and Social Policy. *Children and Society* **3**(1), 67–80

Willmott, P. (1986) *Social Networks, Informal Care and Public Policy*. Policy Studies Institute, London

Yellot, A. (1990) Mediation and domestic violence – a call for collaboration. *Mediation Quarterly* **8**, 5

Zill, N. (1978) *Divorce, Marital Happiness, and the Mental Health of Children: Findings from the FCD National Survey of Children*. Paper presented at the NIMN Workshop on Divorce and Children (Bethesda, MD)

Zill, N. (1982) *Marital Disruption*. Segal & Brim, USA

Zill, N. (1988) Behavior, achievement, and health problems among children in stepfamilies. In E.M. Hetherington & J.D. Arasteh (Eds), *Impact of Divorce, Single Parenting, and Step-parenting on Children*, 324–368. Lawrence Erlbaum (Hillsdale, NJ)